HAMPSHIRE
TALES OF MYSTERY
AND MURDER

HAMPSHIRE
TALES OF MYSTERY
AND MURDER

Ian Fox

COUNTRYSIDE BOOKS
Newbury, Berkshire

First published 2001
© Ian Fox 2001

COUNTRYSIDE BOOKS
3 Catherine Road
Newbury, Berkshire

To view our complete range of books,
please visit us at
www.countrysidebooks.co.uk

ISBN 1 85306 716 4

*Dedicated to my dear grandson George, without whose
countless distractions this book would have been
completed in a fraction of the time.*

Designed by Mon Mohan
Produced through MRM Associates Ltd., Reading
Printed by J.W. Arrowsmith Ltd., Bristol

Contents

THE MYSTERY OF THE
FROGMAN SPY

It took three meetings and considerable tact before a retired Soviet intelligence chief could be persuaded to tell his secrets. The Israeli journalist who interviewed him in Haifa may have resolved one of the great mysteries of the Cold War era — a story of espionage and death which began 2,000 miles away in Hampshire nearly 40 years earlier.

At least ten books, reams of newsprint, several TV documentaries and a film have been devoted to speculation about the disappearance of Commander Lionel 'Buster' Crabb, the British frogman whose abortive spying mission in Portsmouth Harbour threatened to jeopardise Anglo-Soviet relations. Theories about what happened range from the plausible to the bizarre. Many people even doubt that the body buried under a headstone bearing Crabb's name is truly his.

So what did happen to Buster Crabb? There were those who said his mysterious, James Bond-style departure was a fitting end to a career in which danger, intrigue and imminent death were his frequent companions.

To get the answer into perspective means looking back initially to 1942. Crabb, then a lieutenant, was a Royal Navy demolitions officer tackling enemy mines and

Commander Lionel 'Buster' Crabb. Did he drown — or was he murdered by a Russian navy sniper?

unexploded bombs in Gibraltar harbour. They were hair-raising days, diving in navy-issue overalls, plimsolls and submarine escape breathing apparatus, and the dangerous work earned him the George Medal and promotion to lieutenant-commander rank. Equally hazardous postings followed, diving to retrieve and dispose of explosive devices in the ports of north Italy and Palestine, in the course of which he received an OBE.

Crabb spent many of his post-war years on sensitive and sometimes dangerous underwater missions requiring courage, skill and an almost reckless aptitude for taking risks. The few jobs that became public knowledge include his involvement with rescue attempts on the crashed submarines *Truculent* in 1950 and *Affray* the following year. But there were clandestine operations too. Especially significant to the Crabb mystery is a claim that during the Spithead Naval Review in 1955 he recruited another frogman to join him in a secret dive, on behalf of the American CIA, to discover why the Russian cruiser *Sverdlov* was so amazingly manoeuvrable. They found a large opening in the hull through which a bow-thruster propeller could be lowered.

Did the success of this particular piece of underwater espionage seal Buster Crabb's fate? Or was his dive beneath the *Sverdlov* just one of many similar assignments for Western intelligence agencies? Many of us will never know, just as we will never learn the official explanation for his disappearance, because the relevant government papers have been sealed — unusually — until the year 2057. Ordinarily they would have been made public under the 30-year rule in 1986. What is so ultra-sensitive about the Crabb affair?

Despite official reluctance to admit responsibility, there is ample reason to link Crabb's disappearance with a goodwill visit to Britain by the former Soviet leaders Kruschev and

Bulganin. It was a time of mutual distrust between East and West. With the world in fear of a nuclear Armageddon, careful diplomacy was the order of the day. Unsurprisingly, Anthony Eden's government later wrung its hands, claiming to have forbidden any acts of espionage against its guests. Whatever the truth of that, the opportunity for some productive spying proved irresistible in some quarters when it was learned that the Russians would arrive on the cruiser *Ordzhonikidze*. The British and Americans believed the warship's hull to be of revolutionary design, besides having the world's most advanced anti-submarine sonar and special hatches for laying mines. Someone had to go down and take a look.

Ordzhonikidze and two escort destroyers moored at South Railway Jetty in Portsmouth Dockyard on 18 April 1956. Kruschev and Bulganin were whisked away to London while sailors from the Soviet ships partook of the hospitality laid on for them by Portsmouth. Their goodwill visit seemed to go smoothly. Not until the Russians were well away from these shores did the storm break.

The first rumblings were heard towards the end of April, with rumours that Britain's finest frogman, Commander Lionel Crabb, had been lost while diving at Portsmouth. Under increasing media pressure to say something, the Admiralty reluctantly confirmed on 29 April that he was 'missing, presumed drowned'. He disappeared, continued the statement, while diving at Stokes Bay, Gosport, engaged on testing 'certain underwater apparatus'. Any hopes that this cover story would satisfy the hounds of the press were quickly dashed. Sniffing around Portsmouth, the scent they had uncovered was enough to arouse their hunting instincts and they were soon in full cry.

Attention focused on the Sallyport Hotel in Old Portsmouth. Crabb had stayed there overnight on

Tuesday, 17 April in the company of a 'Mr Smith'. (Years later, it was alleged that this was Bernard Smith, a novice agent with the Secret Intelligence Service.) *Ordzhonikidze* arrived on the Wednesday, and that evening Crabb was in Havant, drinking with friends, before catching a train back to Portsmouth. There are reports that early next morning, Thursday, a frogman was seen entering the sea from a beach at the mouth of Portsmouth Harbour, but effectively Crabb had disappeared. 'Mr Smith' settled their bill at the Sallyport Hotel with cash and removed all Crabb's possessions, including his trademark swordstick surmounted with a golden crab.

The press really knew they were on to something when

Buster Crabb and 'Mr Smith' stayed at this Portsmouth hotel immediately before the frogman's mysterious disappearance.

they tried to examine the hotel register. They were too late. Plain-clothes police officers had already been sent to the Sallyport to tear out the details of everyone staying there on the night of the 17th.

Perhaps sensing the opportunity to cause some mischief and embarrassment, on 4 May the Soviets asked the British Foreign Office to explain why a frogman had been spotted by Russian sailors during the Portsmouth visit, swimming between their destroyers. The British reply expressed regret, admitting that it was probably Commander Crabb, who was 'completely unauthorised' to approach the ships. The Prime Minister later declined to tell the House of Commons anything more about Crabb's presumed death. 'It would not be in the public interest,' he said, before adding darkly that 'appropriate disciplinary steps' were in hand. In fact, the head of the SIS was sacked and a special enquiry led to a complete overhaul of secret service internal organisation.

Despite the best efforts of the world's press and investigative journalists for nearly half a century, no one can reliably claim to have uncovered the full story behind what appears to have been a bungled espionage attempt. One of the many questions yet to be answered is whether the 46-year-old veteran was up to the job. Although highly experienced, Crabb was neither fit nor healthy, his constitution weakened by severe alcohol abuse. Was it due to a heart attack, for example, that he prejudiced his mission by surfacing so dangerously close to the Russians?

Some 14 months after Crabb's disappearance (and, it is claimed, just three days after some Russian submarines passed through the English Channel), John Randall was fishing in Chichester Harbour with two friends, Ted and Bill Gilby, when they saw what appeared to be a black tractor tyre floating just below the surface. They managed to drag it into their boat, where it turned out to be the remains of a human corpse in an underwater suit of fairly unusual design. The London manufacturers later confirmed selling an identical one to Crabb, their regular customer, in October 1955. A tight band around the middle of the suit had preserved the body's lower regions, but the upper torso was just a collection of bones and pieces of flesh. The head and hands were missing, as might be expected — they had been exposed to the depredations of marine creatures. There was nothing to indicate the cause of death.

The coroner adjudicated that Commander Lionel Crabb had been found. The remains were buried at Portsmouth's Milton cemetery in July 1957. But instead of drawing a line under the mystery, that gruesome find in Chichester Harbour rekindled the controversy about Crabb's fate. Speculation still rages as to whether the body really was the missing frogman, just as an astonishing number of claims and theories about his disappearance — some of them ridiculous in the extreme — have surfaced over the years. Even the then chief constable of Portsmouth had his say 20 years after the event, alleging that Crabb and Smith arrived at his office unannounced and requested his help with their spying mission. He gave them an office at the police station with a scrambler phone, and on the morning of 19 April a horrified Smith reported in detail to the chief constable how Crabb had entered the water at King's Stairs in the naval dockyard, experienced difficulty with the weights in his diving suit and failed to return, presumably drowned.

But did he drown? What really happened in the murky waters of Portsmouth Harbour? These questions still tax the imagination of authors, journalists and conspiracy theorists. One particularly persistent story has the Soviets kidnapping Crabb on his clandestine dive and taking him to Russia, where he agrees, either voluntarily or under duress, to serve in their navy as Lieutenant (or Commander) Lev Korablov.

Has the truth at last been revealed? As the 20th century drew to its close, a reporter for the Israeli newspaper *Yedioth Ahronoth* sought an interview with a 90-year-old man named Joseph Chwortkin, said to be a former head of Soviet naval intelligence. Chwortkin had immigrated to Israel in 1990 and the word was that he knew what had happened to Crabb. Only at their third meeting did he agree to speak.

The ex-colonel claimed to have been a Soviet undercover agent in England, posing as a German citizen, in 1956. All the stories about Crabb being captured or that he was actually a Russian spy, a double agent, are false, said the old man. 'The truth is much more prosaic. The Soviets discovered Crabb snooping on them and they shot him. I'm not going to tell you whether I was a witness but I know for a fact this is what happened.'

A watchman on the warship, some 60 feet above him, spotted Crabb momentarily come to the surface. He alerted his superiors, who increased the watch and ordered two men to shoot anyone near the ship. One was an ordinary seaman, the other a gunnery officer who was an excellent marksman. They had small-calibre sniper guns. The frogman came up near the ship again and swam on the surface, possibly suffering breathing problems. The officer shot him in the head. He sank and did not reappear.

Could this finally be the definitive answer to the riddle of Buster Crabb? Did his murdered body wash slowly out of the harbour, gradually drifting eastwards to Sussex and a rendezvous with three fishermen? Or is Colonel Chwortkin's unsubstantiated testimony merely the latest twist in an endless saga of intrigue?

East and West have revealed many Cold War secrets. Why, then, do both sides continue to keep silent about Crabb? The disappearance of Portsmouth's frogman spy remains one of the classic mysteries of our time.

THE MURDER STONE

There is a place on a hill above Hambledon that is tainted by evil. People are still known to avoid it after dark, especially if they are on foot and alone and of a nervous disposition. Set among lonely fields, it adjoins a road which was probably little more than a cart-track 200 years ago, when the vile deed was committed. Up here the glow of light from the village in the valley hardly relieves the hushed blackness of night, and in former years, without even the comfort afforded by those distant lights, this would have been a cheerless path to tread.

We can imagine the weary labourer, anxious to be home from the fields at dusk, quickening his pace as he reaches a bend in the track and remembers its awful legacy. Night is falling fast. A keening wind tosses the trees. Something unseen rustles in the grass. Uneasily he hastens past, his gaze averted lest despite the dark he should witness the dreadful spectre of Nicholas Stares rise groaning from the earth with ghastly white face and bloody neck.

Those who passed that way were not allowed to forget the fate of Nicholas Stares. The Murder Stone was there to remind them — as it reminds us today.

For more than two centuries the stone has marked the spot where horrified villagers found a mutilated body. It was early in the morning of Thursday, 22 August 1782. They

For more than 200 years, the Murder Stone has marked the scene of a brutal killing at Hambledon.

faced a sickening sight. The man's corpse had lain by the track for five or more hours, cold to the touch now and beginning to stiffen. Flies swarmed busily around its battered head, feasting. The clothing was sodden with dew and blood and gore.

That Nicholas Stares had been murdered was clear from the outset. Not only had he suffered a violent death but also his attacker had subjected him to a merciless beating. According to one appalled observer, 'It was a cruel murder. His body had been mangled in a most shocking manner.'

Cuts and bruises entirely covered the victim's face and head. Examination of his arm also revealed numerous cuts and other injuries, clear evidence of desperate attempts to ward off repeated forceful blows rained down by his assailant. Most hideous of all were the severe wounds that appeared to have been the main cause of death. A terrible gash had been slashed across the unfortunate man's neck, laying it open from ear to ear, and a further deep cut extended downwards from his chin.

A knife or similar sharp blade, wielded with vicious determination, was the probable cause of those wicked slashes. No such instrument could be found at the scene. But alongside the body the murderer had discarded the remains of what seemed to have been another weapon used during his savage assault. It appeared to be the long wooden handle of a broom or mop, bloodstained now and broken into several pieces by the severity of the attack. Frenzied blows with this pole had doubtless caused all those bruises on his head and arm.

Further examination of the body revealed that the assailant had cut off and stolen the buckles from Stares's shoes. Also missing were the buttons from his coat sleeves. Assuming these ornaments to have been of some value — perhaps they were silver — was this the only motive for so vile a crime? Had a man been bludgeoned and hacked to death for the sake of two shoe buckles and a few buttons? It appeared they would be looking for a callous thief — or a madman.

Once the body had been identified and carried down into Hambledon, tracing the victim's movements prior to his murder proved to be a simple matter. It was ascertained that Nicholas Stares had left his home in the village of Soberton the previous afternoon to walk to Hambledon, a distance of perhaps three or four miles along winding cross-country lanes. The purpose of his journey was to keep an appointment at the New Inn, in the course of which he was due to receive a certain amount of money.

Mr Tribe, landlord of the New Inn, remembered Stares being at his establishment. So did his staff. He had spent a convivial evening there, drinking and discoursing with his acquaintance, in the course of which their business was concluded and the cash passed hands. Whether drink had caused the two men to lower their guard or whether they were simply naïve we do not know, but foolishly their transaction was carried out in full view of other customers at the inn. And for all we know, Mr Tribe may well have had a full house that evening.

Hambledon in August sometimes attracted hundreds, even thousands, of visitors. They came from everywhere to watch the village's famous cricketers. Interest was particularly high in that year of 1782, as the players were in the process of moving from their traditional ground on Broadhalfpenny Down, some three miles from the village, to the nearer Windmill Down — which meant even more trade for licensed victuallers like Mr Tribe.

Large crowds attract pickpockets and thieves. No doubt there were a few such undesirables in the New Inn that August evening. But it was no stranger who greedily watched Nicholas Stares conducting his business and plotted how to deprive him of his cash. It was someone much closer to home.

Seated in the kitchen, also drinking with a friend, was a young man, about 22 years of age, who was well known to Mr Tribe and his other regulars. He was named John Taylor, and he worked as a blacksmith for his mother at her smithy on the Soberton road. What Nicholas Stares did not realise, as he relaxed and perhaps discussed cricket, was that the sight of money changing hands had given young Taylor an extremely unpleasant idea.

By about half past eleven, Stares decided he had had enough. It was time to face the long walk home. As he rose to his feet, somewhat unsteadily perhaps, John Taylor engaged him in conversation and soon made a friendly suggestion. Stares would have to pass Taylor's home, which lay about halfway between the New Inn and Soberton. If they walked together, Stares would have company and protection against the perils of the night for at least some of his way home.

It was nearly midnight before the landlord finally saw the two men leave his premises and set off together into the darkness. As he bade them goodnight, Tribe noticed something unusual. In place of a walking stick, the powerful young blacksmith was carrying the handle of an old mop . . .

Clearly the finger of guilt pointed towards Taylor. He was linked to the victim and to the fatal weapon. The men's journey towards Hoe Cross and the Soberton road would have taken them up Cams Hill to the sharp bend where Stares had met his end. Furthermore, a motive for murder had been established. It was more than a matter of buttons and a couple of shoe buckles — not a penny piece of his money had been found on Stares's corpse.

They traced the blacksmith very quickly that day. At once accused of the killing, Taylor's immediate trembling was taken as an indication of guilt. But under questioning he denied knowing anything about the murder.

Attention turned towards a frock-coat which witnesses remembered him wearing as he left the inn the previous night. Taylor was adamant that they were mistaken. He claimed never to have owned one. A thorough search of his mother's house adjoining her smithy where he worked proved fruitless. Then the searchers moved into the smithy itself. Suddenly, one of the party shouted in triumph as he produced a long-skirted coat from its hiding place behind the forge. Dirt had been rubbed over the coat in an attempt to conceal or remove extensive fresh bloodstains. This was damning evidence.

The frock-coat became the focus of tense exchanges next day during the magistrate's formal examination. A vital link with the killing would be established if it could be proved that Taylor not only owned that bloodstained garment but also had been wearing it when he left the New Inn with Nicholas Stares. Taylor was ordered to put it on. Mr Tribe and his maidservant were then sworn as witnesses and both identified it positively as the one they had seen him wearing that fateful evening.

They were mistaken or lying, insisted Taylor doggedly. It was not his coat, he had never seen it before in his life, nor had he ever owned one remotely like it. But the final witness proved to be his nemesis. It was someone who might be expected to support him to the hilt — his own mother. In the event, Mrs Taylor's religious convictions overcame her protective maternal instincts towards her offspring. Put to the oath and reminded of its sanctity, she was asked point-blank whether or not the frock-coat belonged to her son. Realising the awful significance of her answer but nevertheless respecting her oath, she had to acknowledge that it was indeed his.

In effect, she had signed her son's death warrant. Charged with wilful murder, the blacksmith was committed for trial at the next county assizes. The clocks in Winchester were chiming seven o'clock as he arrived under escort at the county gaol that Friday evening. There he languished for six months until his case came to trial.

On 7 March 1783, at the end of the assize session, it was announced that John Taylor had been found guilty of the wilful murder of Nicholas Stares. A few days later, early on a Monday morning, they took him a mile or so out of the city, probably to Gallows Hill on the Andover to Newbury road, where the crowds used to gather to enjoy the executions. There they put a rope around his neck and hanged him. When the young man was dead they took his body down and without ceremony handed it over to the surgeons 'to be dissected and anatomized' in accordance with his sentence. Such punishment for common murderers had been mandatory for 31 years, ever since Parliament passed 'An Act for the Better Preventing the Horrid Crimes of Murder'. It was intended to deter people like John Taylor.

There the story might have ended. After all, savage though it may have been, the killing of Nicholas Stares was just another murder, to be forgotten as memories faded and old men died. But the Murder Stone still stands by a bend in the road beyond the top of Cams Hill. Even though there is nothing left of the legend once inscribed into its face, which began 'Let future generations know . . .', the stone needs no words to act as a constant reminder of a night when evil was unleashed on a hill above Hambledon.

And if you ask around the village you may still find those who believe that a ghost with a slashed and bloody neck haunts this lonely, tainted place.

THE MYSTERIOUS MR TYRIE

Eng007land in 1782 was a country weakened by military commitments in America, India, the Mediterranean and the West Indies. Across the Channel, strong French and Spanish forces waited to invade her shores. Opposing them was the Royal Navy, overstretched and increasingly reliant on pressed men. And, as invariably happens when a nation is at war, there was also a sinister internal threat to be countered. It came from men who were willing to betray their country's secrets to the enemy — men such as David Tyrie.

No one knows the extent of his spying activities. What damage he did to naval operations and the war effort, the number of ships he indirectly sent to the bottom, how many lives were lost through his perfidy — all these things will for ever be a mystery, like the man himself.

For our purposes, David Tyrie enters this tale of treachery in November 1781, when he approached an old acquaintance by the name of James Mailstone with a most tempting offer. Through his work in the Navy Office at Portsmouth he could arrange lucrative contracts for Mailstone to supply provisions for the East India fleet. When his friend had taken the bait, Tyrie casually mentioned another small matter: he was prepared to pay good money for details of all naval movements in and out of Portsmouth.

Mailstone raised his eyebrows in alarm. This would be valuable intelligence to an enemy. But Tyrie hastened to assure him that of course everything he did was cleared through the Ministry. Mailstone earned more than £30 by this means during the ensuing two or three months, a welcome addition to his income, although Tyrie's persistent demands for more and more information sometimes made him wonder what he had got himself into.

His suspicions hardened when Tyrie one day instructed him to hand his latest lists directly to a sea captain named Bowles — who, he discovered to his consternation, was about to sail for the enemy coast of France 'to load wine for the East India ships'. Nevertheless, he gave the shipping lists to Captain Bowles, then and on several subsequent occasions. As the weeks passed, an increasingly worried Mailstone sometimes delayed handing over his information or even falsified its content, whereas Bowles remained a faithful and regular courier for Tyrie. His smuggling trips to France provided the ideal conduit for espionage.

David Tyrie worked hard to keep the French supplied with useful intelligence. Besides the sensitive information he himself gleaned through his employment at the Navy Office, he had Mailstone's reports and, for all we know, those of other agents who may have been in his employ. Everything was collated before being ferried swiftly across the Channel. Then there came a succession of events that brought the whole enterprise crashing down upon his head.

The beginning of the end was the fateful day when Captain Bowles, the spy's vital link with France, lost his ship as it left Boulogne. Tyrie urgently needed a new courier, so in February 1782 we find him deep in conversation with Captain William James on the beach at Gosport. Perhaps someone had recommended James as a skipper who would not be averse to making a few dishonest pounds. Smuggling was second nature to many seamen. Tyrie knew he had chosen his man wisely when James appeared tempted by his offer of £15 to run a cargo of wine from France. As before, Tyrie's cover story was that this contraband was actually for the East India ships. James weakened even further when told he would be given a letter of credit authorising him to receive a further £50 while in France.

That evening he met Tyrie and his wife by arrangement at the Crown Inn in Gosport, where they had their lodgings. Mailstone was there too, having just handed over some information, and Mr and Mrs Tyrie were both writing furiously. A number of letters lay on the table. James said he would accept the smuggling mission, whereupon Tyrie, assuming this to be confirmation that he was an unprincipled rogue who could be trusted to keep his mouth shut, made a fatal error. He had to get certain intelligence to France as quickly as possible. There was no option but to trust Captain James, who must sail at the earliest opportunity. Tyrie bundled the letters into a packet, which he sealed and handed to his new recruit with instructions to open it once his vessel had cleared the Isle of Wight. He was to deliver the contents 'at Cherbourg or Boulogne, whichever port he could soonest make'. Tyrie also gave James a schedule of secret recognition signals he should make from his ship to avoid being fired on while approaching the French port. A small boat would come out to receive the packet, after which James could sail into harbour and take on his cargo.

Captain James did not leave for France that night. He spent it wrestling with his conscience. Smuggling was one thing but this unexpected additional task had a nasty taste to it. How could Tyrie arrange for him to sail unmolested into an enemy port? The man had to be in league with the French military. In which case, what was in that correspondence he was expected to hand over in France? Next morning he confided his suspicions to a Captain Harrison in Portsmouth, who broke open the packet. What he found inside sent Harrison post-haste to London.

A horrified government official examined Tyrie's letters. One of them, addressed to the Commandant at Cherbourg, gave precise details of a squadron of British ships which had just sailed to intercept a fleet of French supply vessels on its way from Cherbourg to a rendezvous off La Hague. Another letter, to a Monsieur Brodelet via the office of the Minister of Marine in Paris, contained a wealth of information about the movements and stations of various British warships. Potentially most damaging were full particulars of the recent departure of the East and West India convoy fleets from Spithead, including the names of every escorting man-of-war, their exact destinations — even the wind direction. Any French admiral would have given his eye-teeth for such information.

Other letters instructed merchants in Cherbourg and Ostend to provide Captain James with his cargo of wines, spirits and tea. Payment would be arranged through the same Monsieur Brodelet in Paris.

What the authorities could not know as they examined this incriminating material was that the spy's days were numbered anyway. Just a few days previously, Tyrie's wife — who, as we have seen, was his partner in crime — had arrived at the London home of a Mrs Maria Hervey in an understandably bad temper, having travelled, she complained, five hundred miles with three coach changes for the sole purpose of delivering a bundle of papers on behalf of 'a man named Tyrie'. Mrs Hervey knew the woman only by an alias and now she wondered why 'Mrs Askew' was so clearly agitated as she handed over the papers. They related to family matters, she said, and must on no account be seen by anyone. Naturally, the good Mrs Hervey wasted no time in reading them as soon as 'Mrs Askew' had left. Then, thoroughly alarmed by what she had read, she scurried off to have her suspicions confirmed by a male friend.

Tyrie must have taken leave of his senses to entrust such documents, unsealed, to Mrs Hervey. They were dynamite. The bulk of them comprised extensive copies, in Tyrie's handwriting, of entries in current ledgers maintained by the surveyor's branch of the Navy Office, where he worked. They amounted to an up-to-date snapshot of the state of the entire British navy. A contemporary source summarised the material as 'lists of all English ships of war in and out of commission; their different situations and appointments; their present and intended stations; number of ships building, and under repair, in all the different dockyards and merchants' yards in the kingdom'. Damning notes recorded the dates on which Tyrie had forwarded some of these details to addresses in France. Separately listed were warships at Spithead on particular dates. There was also advice to his French masters on sources of information about virtually every aspect of Royal Navy affairs, together with suggestions for establishing an espionage network in the nation's dockyards, including its probable cost in 'salaries' and incidental expenses.

Strong stuff indeed, sufficient to have constables lying in wait at the Hervey residence when 'Mrs Askew' returned from Gosport to collect the papers. Within a few days her husband was also apprehended. Weeks of interrogation failed to extract anything useful from him. Tyrie refused to incriminate anyone else and certainly no evidence of confession was adduced when he faced trial before a special commission at Winchester Castle in August 1782. The two indictments charged high treason. After a remarkably short hearing — it lasted eight hours, during which Tyrie objected to 35 jurors and unsuccessfully requested an adjournment to the next assizes, in order to call four witnesses to prove his innocence — the jury immediately found him guilty.

The law specified dreadful punishment for treason. So it was that Tyrie heard his sentence in the following terms: 'That you be taken to the place from whence you came, and from thence drawn upon a hurdle to the place of execution; you are there to be hung by the neck, but not till you are dead; your privy member shall be cut off, and your bowels taken out while yet alive, and burnt before your face; your head shall be severed from your body, and your body divided into four quarters, and disposed of as His Majesty shall think fit; and the Lord have mercy on your soul.'

Unsurprisingly, Tyrie tried to avoid this hideous death. First he attempted suicide with a razor but was overpowered by his gaolers. Next, awaiting transfer to Winchester from Newgate prison (where initially he was held) in preparation for his execution, he plotted unsuccessfully for a gang of hired ruffians to rescue him from his escort as their carriage passed over Bagshot Heath. Finally, incarcerated in the old county gaol, off Winchester's Jewry Street, he was involved in preparations for a mass break-out.

Using tools that Tyrie paid to have smuggled in, the prisoners laboriously loosened nearly all the bricks through their three-foot-thick dungeon wall. The hole was disguised each morning by a plank, with white cement applied to the crevices to match the surrounding whitewash. Had gaolers not discovered their tunnel, David Tyrie and some of his co-conspirators intended escaping to France.

Instead, he left prison in more conventional fashion at four in the morning on 24 August. Six horses pulled his coach to Portsmouth, the scene of most of his treachery, where he was placed upon a sledge and drawn to the wild place we now call Southsea Common. The traitor had become the focus of a wartime nation's anger, and tens of thousands were there to witness the bogeyman's demise. Grudgingly, they had to acknowledge his courage. He chatted amiably to the gaoler as he was dragged on the sledge, and even as he saw the gibbet, the executioners' glowing brazier and their terrible butcher's implements ready for his torture, Tyrie remained remarkably steadfast and composed. He never hung his head the whole time.

He even joked, chiding his executioners for inattention and neglect when they realised there was no rope for his hanging. Then he stood quietly reading a Bible while, in a moment of farce, a rope and pulley were hastily procured from a nearby lugger and rigged on the gibbet. He declined an invitation to address the crowd with his last words, observing that he failed to see why he should satisfy their idle curiosity.

Then the awful sentence was carried out — literally. They let Tyrie hang for exactly 22 minutes, making sure he did not die. They lowered him onto the sledge and carefully gutted him. They cut off his genitals and his head and they burnt his heart on the fire. They quartered his body. Finally, they dumped his gory remains into a coffin, which they buried in the shingle on the beach.

The Portsmouth sailors he had betrayed now took their own barbarous revenge. Hardly had the mayor and other official witnesses left the scene before the mob tore open the coffin and hacked the remains into a thousand pieces, fighting like wild beasts for a finger, a toe, a fragment of flesh or bloodstained clothing — anything they might keep as a souvenir or talisman. Even hardened reporters were revolted by the sight. Buck Adams, keeper of the Gosport bridewell (lock-up), carried off Tyrie's head, pickled it in spirits and made a few pounds by displaying it as a curiosity.

This 'correct likeness' of David Tyrie was published four days after his barbaric execution.

Later he kept it on the counter of his beerhouse for many years.

Who was David Tyrie? Where did he come from? Why did he seemingly hate England to the extent that he betrayed her secrets to the French? All these questions went unanswered, not least by Tyrie himself. For some reason he considered it important to record, as one of his last acts on earth, a specific written declaration that he had told his life story to nobody. Some people said he was a Scotsman, others that he came from America, whence his father had fled after fighting the English at Culloden. Was Tyrie exacting revenge for the dreadful persecution in Scotland after the 1745 rebellion?

Although his interrogators had failed to loosen his tongue, shortly before his execution Tyrie suddenly offered to reveal several other spies, provided the government promised not to prosecute them. He claimed that they included a very well-placed individual, 'caressed by the first people in this country', with access to the nation's top secrets, who for some time had been passing such information to the enemy. The authorities made a counter offer, hinting at a reprieve from execution if Tyrie named them. Never, he replied; he could not live with the blood of others on his conscience.

Unless all this was bluster, it does appear that he was involved with other spies in this country. His own cross-Channel operations were a success for at least several months. But in other respects, as we have seen, he made enough elementary blunders to cast doubt upon his proficiency and any possible training. Perhaps we will never know whether the mysterious David Tyrie was part of a professional French espionage network, or simply an enthusiastic, resourceful and brave amateur who came to a hideous death through his own foolish mistakes.

THREE DIED — TEN
WERE TRIED

The war had been long and wearisome. Now a cautious optimism was in the air. Exactly four months earlier a great armada had sailed for the Normandy beaches, putting armies ashore on D-Day to chase Hitler's forces across Europe. Everywhere, it seemed, the enemy was withdrawing, with Arnhem almost an irrelevant disaster in the scale of events. Tanks and men now stood poised to cross the borders into Germany and finally bring an end to the conflict.

Hampshire had formed the springboard for the invasion. At times the county seemed like one huge military encampment. Even the abrupt departure of tens of thousands of men for the assault on France provided only a temporary respite. As autumn arrived, Hampshire was still the neck of a funnel supplying the armies across the Channel. Great numbers of troops were forever arriving and leaving and moving between camps. Many of them had been plucked from their homes in America to be shipped to this small foreign island with its strange customs and warm beer.

So it was with the men of 3247 Quartermaster's Service Company, United States Army. They had been based in Devon until 5 October 1944. Early that morning a train brought them to Hampshire, and at 4.30 in the afternoon they arrived at their destination, a tiny hamlet called Sydmonton, near the Berkshire border. Their new camp was at Sydmonton Court, a requisitioned country mansion, where for the first few hours the soldiers were occupied with cleaning the barracks, being assigned to their rooms, bringing in their cot beds and generally settling-in. As was the custom, each man had carried his own weapon — usually a carbine or a longer rifle — during the journey from Devon. They still had them in their barrack rooms that evening, with plenty of ammunition. Not until 10.45 pm were the guns collected from the soldiers' beds for safe storage. By then it was too late.

The American troops based in that part of north Hampshire during the preceding months had not endeared themselves to the authorities. Some of their number were responsible for a serious catalogue of crimes, including murder, rape, burglary and molesting women. Perhaps such outrages were inevitable among an enormous, mainly conscript army, comprising men from all backgrounds and abilities, and to their credit the US military took the problem seriously in their efforts to maintain good relations with the host population. Nevertheless, local magistrates and police chiefs were concerned at a rate of crime hitherto unknown in their rural patch.

Three miles from Sydmonton, the village of Kingsclere offered the nearest opportunity for off-duty relaxation. Its pubs were not exactly buzzing with excitement, but at least they provided alcohol, friendship, the possibility of meeting a girl and the chance to forget military life for a while. On that first evening at Sydmonton Court, the lure of these simple pleasures proved sufficient to persuade several of the new arrivals to ignore two inconvenient facts. First, none of them had passes authorising them to leave camp. Second, the Provost Officer had instructed that any off-duty troops visiting Kingsclere must wear Class A uniforms – their best — and some of the men had not even been issued with them.

Sneaking out of barracks, small groups of soldiers walked or hitchhiked along the narrow country road that led to the comforts of Kingsclere. Among them were Private Coleman Binns and Private First Class (PFC) James Agnew. Arriving in Kingsclere, they soon discovered the Bolton Arms. Two men from their company were already drinking in the pub and a group of six others soon arrived also. They were set for an enjoyable evening — but to everyone's considerable annoyance, three or four American military policemen followed the group into the pub.

A number of auxiliary military police had been deployed to patrol Kingsclere as part of the drive against disorder by US troops. Pte Binns and his buddies, wearing field jackets instead of the compulsory Class A uniform, were bound to attract their attention.

An acrimonious exchange followed as the MPs ordered the soldiers to return to camp because they were improperly dressed and in any case had no passes. The attitude of one MP, a short man, particularly enraged the group. At some stage a policeman cocked his rifle, which did nothing to ease the tension. In the event they were allowed to remain in the Bolton Arms until one of their number had finished his drink, after which they left as ordered at about 8.15 pm, hitched a lift in a truck, picked up two more comrades and returned the three miles to barracks.

A wild plan was hatched in the back of that truck. Intense anger over a ruined evening and their treatment at the hands of the MPs fuelled the ringleaders' bravado. 'We should go back to town and take care of them,' someone exclaimed. 'Yeah, especially the little guy who caused so much trouble,' said another. Agreement was reached. They would find the

MPs and beat them up. But the policemen were armed, which prompted Pte Hildreth Fleming to make a fatal suggestion. Why not take their own weapons and ammunition from the barracks to disarm the MPs?

The only sensible man in the back of that truck was Pte Binns. The dangerous talk he heard in the darkness led him to report his fears to his sergeant, after which he went straight to bed. The decision probably saved him from ruining his life. And had the sergeant acted promptly a tragedy might have been prevented.

No one knows for certain how many soldiers took their carbines from alongside their cots, loaded clips with ammunition and set off back to Kingsclere. There were at least eight, possibly more. Not all of the group understood what was going on. One of them, Corporal John Lilly, had been celebrating his birthday and was half drunk. Pte Willie Crawford saw 'some of the boys' walking out of camp and decided to tag on. He had not even been in the village earlier; neither did he have his weapon with him. At first they told Crawford that they only intended 'talking to' the MPs. But after a passing truck picked up the group their conversation took an ominous turn.

Somebody asked whether everyone had brought ammunition. The replies were in the affirmative. They all agreed to load their guns before reaching Kingsclere. Then Pte Ernest Burns said, 'Let's kill the MP.' And from the darkness, PFC Agnew replied, 'No, let me kill him.'

Was murder really their intention? Or were those threats 'just the boys talking', as Crawford supposed? He remained uncertain as the truck pulled into Kingsclere but nevertheless he chose to stay with the gang of armed soldiers. After a brief conference they set out to tour the dark village, hunting their quarry, loaded carbines at the ready. At each pub, because he had no rifle, Willie Crawford was sent in to enquire as to the whereabouts of the MPs.

The soldiers visited the Bolton Arms and the Swan before arriving at the Crown Inn, which stands on the corner of North Street, opposite the parish church. Crawford went into the public bar. He asked about the MPs. They were in the other bar, said someone. The time was nearly ten o'clock — closing time.

Frank Napper had been licensee of the Crown for some nine years. The American troops liked his pub because it was well conducted, they were never overcharged and his 64-year-old wife Rosa, often known as Rose, was very kind and motherly and willing to do anything for them. This was appreciated particularly by the black soldiers stationed in the area — they included the men of 3247 Company and the auxiliary MPs — who enjoyed in Kingsclere a welcome freedom from the prejudice so often experienced in the States. There had been quite a few of them in the pub that evening, happily drinking and playing bar games with the locals.

All was peaceful as closing time approached. In the public bar, Nelson Miles and Frank Butler had just finished their last game of shove ha'penny and were chatting with two other Kingsclere men while watching a couple of GIs play bar billiards. Two or three other soldiers sat on benches, finishing their drinks. 'It was all nice and quiet at three minutes to ten,' Fred Jewell remembered later. 'Not a word had been said out of place.' Mr and Mrs Napper exchanged pleasantries with their customers as they collected the glasses. Relaxing in the other bar were eight or nine soldiers — and two MPs.

Was Willie Crawford the Judas who told them that they were wanted outside? Probably. He admitted later that by the time he left through the front door the MPs had already gone onto the forecourt, to find themselves facing a group of armed, hostile soldiers. It was a tense situation. Crawford

The Crown at Kingsclere, its appearance little changed since the senseless killings in October 1944.

heard the MPs ordering 'disband arms'. One of the policemen began to take his carbine from his shoulder. His colleague, PFC Jacob Anderson, had no weapon, only a flashlight.

A single shot rang out. Which of the soldiers fired it was never satisfactorily established, but it sparked madness. Almost immediately all hell was let loose. Every soldier in the group seemed to be firing his carbine towards the Crown. Bullets smashed into the pub wall, into window frames and through the glass. Others struck two adjoining cottages. Willie Crawford, in the line of fire, hit the ground and survived, later running back to Sydmonton Court in panic.

PFC Anderson took a bullet in the chest. He slumped against the Crown before managing to stagger about 150 yards down North Street, where he collapsed in Mr Digweed's garden, crying for help. Digweed's married daughter, Mrs Mothersell, coming home with a girl friend, heard his moans and quickly called her father, but they could do nothing. A bullet had shattered the MP's breastbone, passed through a lung and penetrated the pulmonary artery. As they watched, Jacob Anderson suffocated in his own blood.

Back at the Crown, his comrade MP had dived safely into the private bar at the first shot. Many of the other customers had hit the floor instinctively upon hearing the sound. The ensuing fusillade brought panic as bullets whizzed into the premises. Several of the shots, it seemed, came from behind tombstones in the churchyard opposite the pub. Other soldiers fired from the dark roadway. Some of the customers ran about like hares, utterly terrified. Others crawled for cover. The two bar billiards players dived under their table. A sergeant was wounded in the face. Another soldier took a bullet through his hand.

Pte Joseph Coates had been sitting in the public bar, beneath a window overlooking North Street. As he leapt up from the chair a bullet went through his temple, fracturing his skull, lacerating his brain. Coates died almost immediately. In the confusion, someone hurled himself through the same window, taking all the glass with him.

Mr and Mrs Napper were stacking beer glasses behind the bar. Splinters of broken glass cut into the landlord's wrist — but he was more concerned for his wife. Diving for the floor, trying to get her down with him, Fred Napper heard Rosa scream as a bullet hit her in the neck. Then she fell by his side, shocked and bleeding.

As the echoes of their one murderous fusillade died away,

most of the offenders scattered into the darkness. At a time of acute petrol shortage, Rosa Napper had to wait about an hour, tended by a local doctor, before eventually an American command car took her to Newbury Hospital. The bullet had passed completely through her neck and the base of her tongue, also shattering her jawbone. Now the tongue was swelling, blocking her windpipe. Despite an emergency tracheotomy, she died at 4.55 am.

Three people had been killed in a moment of senseless mayhem. It was a huge embarrassment for the Americans. Within 48 hours, General Eisenhower sent his second-in-command to Kingsclere to convey Ike's personal regrets and assurances of appropriate action. By then a joint operation by Hampshire and American CID officers had resulted in the arrest of several soldiers.

Forensic tests proved that of 33 spent cartridge cases found at the scene, 15 had been fired from a carbine issued to PFC Willie Washington — a man of the lowest mental grade acceptable for military service. Six rounds were traced to Agnew, the soldier who had wanted to kill an MP.

On 9 and 10 November, five weeks after the shootings, a US Court Martial at Thatcham in Berkshire tried ten soldiers, including Agnew, Crawford, Washington, Fleming and Burns. Each man faced identical charges of jointly murdering the three deceased, jointly engaging in 'a disorderly and riotous assembly of soldiers', and being absent without leave. None of the prisoners seemed much concerned during the proceedings, despite facing the death penalty. Within hours the air in the small room was hot, foul and soporific. No windows were open and everyone smoked furiously at each interval during the hearing. Two of the accused actually dropped off to sleep.

The court found nine men guilty of all charges. Surprisingly perhaps, they escaped execution. Still their sentences were severe: dishonourable discharge from the Army, forfeiture of all pay and allowances, and imprisonment with hard labour for the term of their natural lives.

The tenth accused was Pte Herbert Lawton. He had been charged because his rifle was found at the Crown, having fired seven rounds, although he denied being present during the incident. Accepting his defence that another of the accused, probably PFC John Lockett, had taken his carbine in error, the court acquitted Lawton of the two most serious charges.

But consider this. Simply for being absent without leave for half an hour, from 9.30 to ten o'clock, Herbert Lawton received a dishonourable discharge from the US Army — and ten years' imprisonment with hard labour.

MURDER MOST ROYAL

Is it true that Edgar, the first man to be made king of all England, murdered his friend in a north Hampshire forest? If so, he sparked a calamitous chain of events which altered the course of our nation's history. Had it not been for his bloody deed and its turbulent aftermath, perhaps the Danish king Canute would never have ruled England as part of his great Scandinavian empire and we might not have experienced the reign of Edward the Confessor, who gave us Westminster Abbey.

Even more important to our destiny as a nation, Harold Godwinson might never have been elected to succeed the Confessor in 1066, giving William of Normandy cause to invade our shores so decisively. Were the Norman Conquest and all its momentous consequences the indirect result of a Hampshire murder?

Edgar, great-grandson of the mighty Alfred, was only 15 when he became the first ruler of a united England in AD 959. He worked with his trusted counsellor, the powerful Dunstan, Archbishop of Canterbury, bringing order to State and religious affairs, to the general relief and acclaim of the people. Monasticism was restored, a fleet of ships was organised to deter further attacks by the Norsemen and the vital process of reconciling the country's warring tribes was completed. So it was that he became known as Edgar the Peaceful, or the Peaceable.

But there was a wilder side to this wise young king. Edgar, it seems, had both a mercurial temper and an extremely active libido — common traits in great leaders. No doubt taking advantage of his position, he found enormous pleasure in scandalous behaviour that would have seen any of his subjects punished severely by the very courts he himself had established. The old chroniclers tell tales of seduction and worse, sometimes involving nuns.

He chose as his wife a woman whose beauty had earned her the name of Ethelfled the Fair. Their brief marriage ended in tragedy when she died shortly after giving birth to their only child, leaving Edgar a widower in his early twenties with a son named Edward, who — significantly for our story — was his natural heir.

Edgar was not one to mourn a wife over-long. He continued to enjoy the pleasures of his rank, especially the popular pastimes of riding, feasting, and hunting in the extensive forests that covered much of Wessex. Like other robust young men, he found the most agreeable companions were those who shared his interests, and like most kings he had his favourites at his court in Salisbury. Chief among them was his childhood friend Ethelwold, a lusty East Anglian nobleman, who became the King's trusted confidant and constant companion when he caroused or took to the saddle with hawk and hound.

So it was Ethelwold, his closest friend, to whom Edgar entrusted a special task, a mission so delicate, secret and important that he was forbidden to discuss it with anyone save the King himself. In brief, Ethelwold was to make the first selection of England's new queen.

Reports had reached the King's ears that Elfrida, only daughter of the powerful Earl Ordgar, Ealdorman of Devon and Somerset, was one of the most beautiful women in the realm. If that were the case, and also bearing in mind her father's wealth and his standing among the other English ealdormen, a marriage with the lovely Elfrida might prove to be politically advantageous as well as personally rewarding. But Edgar needed confirmation that she was as desirable as had been reported.

For some reason he chose not to travel to the West Country to meet his potential bride personally. Perhaps matters of state meant he could not spare the time or maybe diplomatic considerations made it inexpedient for him to visit Earl Ordgar. Whatever the cause, Edgar decided to send his friend Ethelwold to Ordgar's Devon stronghold on the pretext of bearing the King's greetings and best intentions to the fiercely independent old earl. But in truth his mission was to assess the daughter's marriage prospects and report them to Edgar.

Every mile of that journey took Ethelwold closer towards his fate. It came in the form of Elfrida herself, for when the ambassador delivered his King's compliments to Ordgar and was in turn introduced to the earl's daughter, he discovered to his delight that her reputation for beauty, intelligence and social grace was entirely justified. Ethelwold found himself smitten by her charms. He fell in love with her and she, unaware of the true reason for his visit, appears to have repaid his affections.

Love is notorious at making fools of intelligent men. It can only have been blind passion that prompted Ethelwold to decide upon a dangerous scheme whose inevitable discovery would have been obvious to any rational thinker. His duty to Edgar, both as a trusted friend and in his capacity as a courtier, was to confirm Elfrida's suitability to be his wife and queen. Instead, in an act of gross betrayal which he must have known was bound to be revealed in due course, his report was exactly the opposite — Elfrida, he told Edgar upon returning to Salisbury, had neither beauty nor charm. His advice was that the King should look elsewhere for a bride.

Ethelwold's ultimate folly was to secretly marry Elfrida, returning with his new wife to his castle at Wherwell in Hampshire. It was the act of a man made reckless by love, someone who perhaps gambled on the hope that Edgar's long absences in other parts of his kingdom meant that he might never meet Elfrida. For her part, Elfrida appears to have been content with her marriage to a powerful and influential nobleman, particularly as she had no idea that she might have been queen.

It could not last. Wherwell was too close to Salisbury, and court gossip soon made mention of this beautiful woman who had become Ethelwold's wife. Edgar's suspicions were aroused. Had not his friend told him that Elfrida was only moderately attractive and unworthy of a King's attention? Was it possible that his closest confidant had betrayed him? There was a sure way to discover the truth.

We can imagine the fear that seized Ethelwold when Edgar announced his intention of visiting his friend's estate at Wherwell to hunt boar in the nearby forest of Harewood — a visit, he added, which would also give him the pleasure of meeting the charming wife of whom he had heard such glowing reports.

Returning in despair to Wherwell, Ethelwold hit upon a possible solution to his parlous situation. It meant making a clean breast to his wife but surely their love would ensure her co-operation. He told Elfrida the whole sorry story, of the secret mission Edgar had given him, of how he had himself fallen for her, and the full extent of his duplicity towards the King. He sought her understanding and forgiveness, then pleaded that she could help to save him from the King's wrath. He urged her to conceal her assets while Edgar was under their roof, perhaps by wearing unflattering robes, pretending to be ignorant of the social graces and altering her appearance so as to appear less attractive. The King must not be allowed to appreciate what a prize he had missed.

What went through Elfrida's mind as she heard her husband's plea? Was it fury at the realisation that without his lies she might have been Edgar's queen, the most powerful and admired woman in all England? Heaven truly has no rage like love to hatred turned, and now it was Elfrida's turn for treachery. But at first she hid her feelings, promising to support Ethelwold by seemingly agreeing with his plan.

Her revenge proved devastating. When Elfrida emerged to welcome the King to Wherwell, it was at once apparent to her husband that, far from dressing down, she had made particular efforts to display her charm and beauty to the full. And as they dined that evening she used every feminine wile to impress and perhaps even to captivate Edgar, who concealed from his host something of which Ethelwold must have been painfully aware — the realisation that his deceit had been exposed.

All was bustle and laughter next morning as the King's hunting party assembled with their horses and hounds. Edgar, it seems, had still given no intimation of his displeasure, so Ethelwold probably took his customary place at his friend's side as the hunt rode into Harewood Forest in search of boar. What none of them knew — maybe not even the King at that stage — was that their day's sport was destined to come to an abrupt and horrific end.

Perhaps Edgar had harsh words with Ethelwold in the forest, confronting him with his perfidy and accusing him of treachery and abuse of friendship. Perhaps he flew into a wild rage, losing control of his actions, or perhaps he simply acted in cold blood and with premeditation. There have been suggestions also that he was prompted not by anger but only by envy and lust, a determination to rob Ethelwold of his lovely wife. None of this is recorded. What we do know, according to the ancient chronicler who left us this story, is that King Edgar suddenly and violently stabbed his erstwhile friend in the back, probably with his hunting spear or possibly with a knife. Ethelwold fell to the ground in agony, only for Edgar to wheel his horse and urge it to trample the wretched man as he lay on the forest floor, until its heavy hooves had pounded the last spark of life from Ethelwold's shattered body.

News of the crime soon reached Dunstan, Archbishop of Canterbury and very much the power behind the throne. His response was worthy of any political spin-doctor. The King's reputation had to be safeguarded. Subtly, Dunstan moved to divert blame away from Edgar, placing it instead upon Elfrida's shoulders. It was she, he let it be known in the land, who had plotted her husband's death and so it was she who must be held responsible.

To the archbishop's annoyance, however, Edgar opposed all attempts to blame Elfrida. He had other plans for the lovely widow. Before her husband's corpse had been in the ground a twelve-month, Edgar and Elfrida were married, and so at last she was queen.

Their marriage was destined to last but eight years, during which time Elfrida bore a son, Ethelred, and Edgar's belated coronation as King of all England took place at Bath. Two years later, in July 975, he died, carried off by a fever while journeying to Glastonbury, where he was buried.

Now was a time for opportunism and dark thoughts. Edgar's sons each had claim to the English throne. Both were mere boys, living under Queen Elfrida's roof in the royal castle at Corfe in Dorset. Edward, who it will be remembered was Edgar's son by his first wife, had reached the age of 13. His coarse manners and abrasive conduct had antagonised many influential people. The other boy, Ethelred, was aged just seven, but thanes loyal to his mother, Elfrida, were prepared to hail him as king. At a time when it was customary for the monarch to be chosen by election, rather than for the eldest son to succeed by right of birth, Elfrida hoped that her boy might yet take the throne, perhaps with herself at his side, but her efforts to rally support for Ethelred's cause were dashed by her old enemy, Archbishop Dunstan.

Shrewdly realising the danger facing young Edward if he remained with his stepmother and her cronies, Dunstan had the boy spirited away from Corfe to safety. Then, due largely to the archbishop's considerable influence, the lords of the Witan chose Edward as their new king and cheered his coronation at Kingston.

Edward's short reign was marred, and tragically ended, by dissent between his followers and those loyal to Elfrida and her son. On 18 March 978, when he had been just three years on the throne, the 15-year-old king called at Corfe Castle to visit his stepmother and half-brother, Ethelred, after a day's hunting. Unwittingly, he had delivered himself into the hands of his enemies. Later that day, young King Edward was murdered at Corfe, probably by thanes who wanted Ethelred on the throne. They concealed his body in a thicket where it lay undiscovered until the following February. 'Worse deed was never done among the English,' lamented the chronicler.

What part, if any, did Elfrida play in the murder of Edward the Martyr? There were those (and to what extent Dunstan encouraged such thoughts is debatable) who believed she had instigated the killing or even stabbed the

boy king herself. One version of the story has her meeting
Edward at the gates of Corfe Castle, smilingly offering him
wine, only to stab him in the back as he leans down to take
the stirrup cup. It was in expiation of her sins, said Elfrida's
detractors, that she founded two nunneries, the first at
Amesbury soon after her stepson's murder and another a
few years later at Wherwell, where she herself took the veil.
And when, after many years of piety and good works, she
was found drowned in a stream at Wherwell, the tongue-
waggers said the burden of her guilt had caused her to take
her own life.

Other scholars have argued recently that Elfrida was
blameless. Furthermore, they say, William of Malmesbury's
12th-century story alleging that King Edgar murdered

*Colonel Iremonger's monument to murder at Deadman's Plack
in Harewood Forest, near Wherwell.*

Ethelwold at Wherwell is equally spurious. Whatever the truth, history records the torment and eventual collapse of the embryo English nation during the dreadful 35-year rule of Elfrida's son. We remember him as Ethelred the Unready.

One man in particular believed the ancient tale. In Harewood Forest, 'upon a spot beyond time of memory called Deadman's Plack', Colonel Iremonger from Wherwell Priory caused to be erected in 1825 a great stone cross, 70 ft high, whose inscription recorded the moment when Edgar slew Ethelwold at that very place. Iremonger's monument to folly and murder stands hidden in the quiet Hampshire forest to this day.

DOWN IN THE FOREST . . .

We only ever knew him as 'the captain'. His workplace had been the world's oceans. Now he enjoyed retirement in his home town of Lymington, where most evenings he could be found at the pub, sitting quietly over a pint in his favourite corner. Despite spending most of his life at sea, the captain had forgotten more about the New Forest than most people will ever know, which is why he was able to tell us about a bizarre forest mystery — the tall man who somehow managed to be in three places at once.

Our conversation in the pub one evening had drifted into speculation about events unusual, improbable or downright inexplicable. From there it was a short step to the supernatural. Someone recalled that more than half of all recorded 'ghosts' are actually apparitions of living individuals, not dead ones. Apparently, a full ten per cent of people who took part in a major survey claimed to have seen a ghost at some time in their lives. That in itself was remarkable. But most of them recognised the phantom as someone who was alive at the time, somewhere else. So is it possible, we wondered, for the image of a living person to be transmitted through space — a kind of natural television?

That was when the captain invited himself into our conversation. There was a funny business at Brook before the war that could have been just like that, he said. Then he told us as much of the tale as he could remember, after which we had to agree it was indeed a peculiar affair.

Perhaps detecting a touch of scepticism in his audience, he added, 'You don't have to accept my word for it. The newspapers wrote about it at the time.'

And he was right. Several years later I came across an old article by E.A. Mitchell, a seasoned journalist who wrote a weekly column for the *Southern Daily Echo* under the pseudonym of 'Townsman'. His headline shot me back in time. 'Were These People Real?' it asked, and beneath that: 'The Tall Man of Brook . . .'

The strange story reported by Mitchell was almost exactly as the captain had remembered. It happened between the wars, a period when people routinely undertook quite lengthy bicycle journeys, private motor transport being a rarity. Betty Bone, a young woman possibly in her late teens or early twenties judging by her photograph, was staying in Breamore, a village near Fordingbridge in the New Forest. She sometimes cycled to Southampton to visit her family, a round trip of some 32 miles. Unfortunately, her journeys along the quiet forest roads had been spoiled recently by a band of gypsies who demanded money from passers-by and threatened violence when refused. Hearing about this upon her arrival in Southampton one weekend in May 1924, her father arranged for Betty to be escorted back to Breamore by her brother and his friend, Ewart Pope. They too are pictured in the newspaper and appear to have been in her age bracket.

It was a fine, clear Sunday evening when the three young people set off from Southampton on their bicycles. Twilight was still an hour or so away as they cycled past Cadnam to pick up the road that runs through the New Forest to Fordingbridge. Nowadays it's the B3078. Nothing seemed untoward until they were opposite the entrance to

Bramshaw golf links, roughly a quarter of a mile beyond the Bell Inn at Brook. The road was empty; there were few motor vehicles on minor forest roads in those days. Visibility was good, even though the cyclists were coming up to an avenue of trees, so they were startled to find themselves suddenly about to overtake a man who was walking in their same direction.

Several things were unusual. In the first place, for some strange reason none of them had noticed the pedestrian until they were only about 20 yards from him. 'He just appeared,' was how they described it. Next, his height. They all agreed later that the man was exceptionally tall — at least seven feet, said one of the trio. No, he was even taller than that, thought another, so lofty it seemed he must have been on stilts. Then there was his clothing. The tall man was wearing a long coat, similar it seems to a frock-coat (we are told it suggested certain pictures of the Charles Dickens character, Mr Micawber), and a tall, brimmed hat, like an antiquated top hat.

Striding purposefully in the direction of Fordingbridge, he was certainly a peculiar sight. For all that, the three young people sailed past him on their cycles without glancing back, so none of them saw his face. That might have been the end of the matter had not a curious event followed.

They had travelled roughly another quarter of a mile and were approaching the top of Telegraph Hill — when precisely the same thing happened. From nowhere, it seemed, the tall man was there again, about 20 paces ahead on a clear road and still walking steadily forwards. From his height and clothing there was no doubt that he was the identical man they had passed previously. But of course it was impossible. There was no way he could have overtaken them. They would have noticed him and anyway their speed was much greater than his.

A contemporary drawing shows the Tall Man of Brook near the entrance to Bramshaw golf course.

Understandably, his sudden reappearance shook the trio, who all confessed later to having felt a sense of unease as they pedalled past at quite a pace. Again, none of them saw his face. But an even greater surprise awaited them further up the road.

About a quarter of a mile beyond Telegraph Hill, which was where they had passed the man for the second time, the forest gave way to almost completely open country with very few trees bordering the road, making visibility even better than before. It was not twilight, let alone dusk. The three cyclists were approaching a crossroads where the left turn leads to Fritham and the right to Nomansland when, to their utter amazement, he suddenly appeared in front of them for a third time.

One moment they were cycling along a road that was empty as far as the eye could see, the next they were behind the same tall man as he strode in a determined manner towards some distant destination. And, as on the previous two occasions, the mysterious figure appeared to be as substantial as any mortal man.

How was it possible for one person to be in three places at virtually the same time? And how could he suddenly appear in their path where previously they had seen nothing? All three later agreed that this was the moment they became thoroughly alarmed and pedalled furiously to get past the strange being in the shortest possible time.

Having delivered Betty Bone safely at Breamore, the two young men braved the return journey through the darkening forest. Although in later years they were able to laugh as they told their tale, they admitted that at the time their nerves were on edge. Even when the lamp fell from one of their bicycles they preferred to pedal on, rather than to stop and pick it up.

Who or what was the Tall Man of Brook? No one knows. There have been no further recorded sightings, but when interviewed 14 years later the three cyclists, by then married and with no cause to maintain any pretence, remained adamant that for a few minutes on a lonely forest road they had encountered something entirely baffling.

THE PHANTOM RIDER
OF BRAMSHOTT

Gaston Lefevre might have lived to return to his native France had his brain not been addled by love. Maybe his family back home could have arranged an exchange for some British naval officer held in similar circumstances on the other side of the Channel. Perhaps, as seemed possible when the news first reached England, Nelson's victory at Trafalgar might have brought peace, followed by repatriation for all French prisoners of war. None of these things happened. Instead, Gaston followed the path trodden by other hot-blooded young men through the ages. He allowed his heart to rule his head and paid a cruel price.

This, of course, supposes that Lieutenant Lefevre and his sweetheart Charlotte Newholme did exist. It is only fair to admit from the outset a complete lack of evidence to support the following tale, which nevertheless was told to me in good faith. Presumably it has some factual foundation. Why else should my informant's grandmother have passed the story down to her? All I have done is to put a little extra flesh on the bones of grannie's yarn, which begins with the capture of young Lefevre in a sea engagement off Cherbourg early in 1805.

It must have been humiliating for a 21-year-old French

lieutenant to see his captain strike his colours and allow a British prize crew on board to take their frigate into Portsmouth roads. From the anchorage at Spithead they were taken off and rowed shorewards under jeers from the British fleet. Their boats separated inside the harbour, the lower ranks bound for the nine stinking prison hulks off Portchester while Gaston and his brother officers spent their first night on English soil in the ancient castle, where to his surprise he slept soundly.

In the morning a Royal Navy captain discussed with them in passable French the question of parole. In essence, it meant the officers would enjoy comparative freedom if they promised on their honour neither to escape nor to engage in hostile acts while on British soil. It was the custom of the time. At sea and abroad, well-bred men of both nations were intent on killing one another. Taken prisoner and put on parole, they behaved and were treated with civility and courtesy. The alternative was confinement in less pleasant circumstances.

Gaston Lefevre was content to give his word. Within days he found himself in a coach which rumbled across the Hampshire countryside before depositing him and other captured officers outside a busy inn called the Royal Anchor in a place he had never heard of. A harassed billeting officer told him its name was Liphook.

The billet he had found for Gaston lay a mile or so away, near a pleasant village known as Bramshott. Mr Jolliffe, into whose home he was introduced, turned out to be an educated man of some means, a pacifist who welcomed the chance to practise his French on the genuine article. Mrs Jolliffe ensured his comfort, while their son William — an athletic lad of about the same age — soon accepted Gaston as a friend rather than a rival in the household.

So it was that a French lieutenant reconciled himself to a

life of ease in the Hampshire countryside while waiting for the war to end. Bound by his word of honour, Gaston often rode alone on horses from the Jolliffes' stables, enjoying the sun on his face. At other times he hunted game with William or fished for trout in the river which crossed the meadows close to the big house. He introduced the family to the game of boules and they tried to teach him the rules of cricket.

If Gaston could have remained content with such pursuits, three lives might never have been wasted in a night of horror and bloodshed — and a tortured spirit would not have been condemned to haunt the lanes of Bramshott for eternity.

But Lefevre was a healthy young man, full of energy and natural drives. As the lazy summer months passed, he often strolled into Liphook to enjoy the bustle around the coaching inns and the sight of young women. So it was that one fateful afternoon he found himself by chance outside a large house that had been converted into a seminary for young ladies. As the front door opened to release a dozen or more girls into the late-August sunshine, Gaston first saw Charlotte Newholme and she him. They probably fell in love at that very instant.

Charlotte had just turned 18 years of age. Her father was one of the wealthier farmers in the area. He was anxious to see Charlotte schooled in the social niceties with a view to her making an advantageous marriage, which is why each day a maidservant drove her into Liphook in a trap to attend the seminary. Several promising young men were already earmarked as potential husbands. A foreign naval lieutenant — an enemy of his country and probably impecunious — had no place in Mr Newholme's plans.

Most days found Gaston loitering near the seminary. Autumn was approaching before he plucked up courage to pass a note in painfully composed English to the maidservant as she waited with the Newholmes' trap. Had he but realised, Charlotte would have welcomed his move weeks before. Now her heart pounded as a daily clandestine correspondence developed between them. Her maidservant, their amused go-between, was sworn to secrecy. So was William Jolliffe, in whom Gaston had confided while underlining his honourable intentions towards Charlotte.

The couple met once, briefly, when the Frenchman conspired to be riding in a lonely lane down which she passed each day. It was a highly dangerous encounter. They scarcely had time for introductions, she blushing prettily and he stammering in poor English, before a gig came into view around the bend. Gaston immediately rode off — too late to avoid being recognised by its driver, a mean-spirited individual who later took pleasure in enquiring casually of Mr Newholme whether he approved of his daughter conversing with Frenchmen in quiet lanes.

Newholme was not the sort of man to fly into a rage. Nevertheless, he was determined to protect his Charlotte, from herself as much as from marauding Frenchies. Was there something going on behind his back? He summoned the maidservant and under threat of taking her job obtained the full story. A tearful interview with his daughter followed. When Charlotte's hopeless infatuation became obvious, Newholme resolved to put some distance between the lovelorn couple in the hope their ardour might cool. First he packed the girl off to stay with her older brother who farmed near Bentley, some eight miles distant from Bramshott. Then he paid a visit to the local military commander, a man whom he had often entertained to dinner. Now was the time to call in a few favours.

The upshot of their conversation was that Lieutenant Lefevre found himself being forced to accept an amendment to his parole. Until further notice he was upon his honour not to leave the confines of Jolliffe's estate. It was a shattering blow for a young man so hopelessly in love. He could see no future if he were to be barred from furthering his courtship. William Jolliffe tried to console his friend, even discovering where Charlotte was staying and obtaining frequent reports about her health and conduct, which Gaston received avidly. Apparently she had confided in friends how she too was devastated by their enforced separation.

Within two weeks Gaston resembled a caged wild animal, bound not by bars but by something equally strong — his parole. His simmering frustration would require very little to explode into irrational action. An event far from Bramshott proved to be the catalyst.

Rumours of Nelson's decisive victory at Trafalgar were soon confirmed by newspaper accounts of the action. Napoleon's invasion plans were shattered along with his fleet. Mastery of the Channel now lay with the British. Coaches stopping at Liphook brought the gossip from London and Portsmouth; it hinted that secret peace talks were already in progress. The war could soon be over, the prisoners on their way home within weeks or even days. For Lefevre, listening in disbelief as William Jolliffe excitedly relayed what he had heard in the village, this was dreadful news.

He wrestled with his conscience for many hours before reaching a decision. His love for Charlotte and the awful possibility that he might never see her again had to take precedence over his parole. It was an agonising decision for a man of honour.

On a foul October night, Gaston Lefevre slipped from the slumbering house and made his way in torrential rain to a nearby copse where young Jolliffe waited with a white horse. William was recently returned from Bentley, where on a supposedly social visit he had made certain secret arrangements with Charlotte Newholme. Now he wished his friend God speed as the young Frenchman rode northwards to keep his midnight tryst.

The barn where Charlotte and Gaston spent their first and last night together was dangerously close to her brother's farmhouse. It was the only place she could suggest for an illicit meeting. What did that young couple speak of as they lay in the straw and listened to the storm lashing their shelter? No doubt they declared their devotion one for the other, railed against an uncaring world and whispered wild, desperate plans for the future. Perhaps they made love. Let us hope they found some happiness.

Investigators on behalf of the coroner later pieced together the following theory about what happened next. Charlotte told them some of it before she died. William Jolliffe sketched in the rest of the background, once he had recovered from his grief and feelings of guilt at his complicity. About an hour before daybreak, Gaston had prepared to leave the barn, determined to be back in Bramshott before his parole breach was discovered. But Charlotte's brother, having risen early for market, surprised them in their last embrace. The outraged farmer immediately launched a fierce attack upon Gaston, slashing open his arm with a billhook. Forced to defend himself against what was clearly a homicidal assault, the Frenchman fought back, using a pitchfork that lay to hand. Whether by accident or design, Newholme was run through and died.

Charlotte pleaded with Gaston to escape. Her brother's death would be blamed on some intruder. Gaston swiftly bade her adieu and rushed out into the rain and darkness, not knowing that she had followed to watch him leave. So it was that when a foolish servant fired from the house into the yard, believing from the commotion that he was shooting at escaping thieves, the ball smashed into her body.

Gaston assumed the fire was directed at him and kept running to the wood where his horse was tethered. Ignorant of his lover's fatal injury, his aim now was to reach Bramshott before the Jolliffe household awoke. He knew he had broken his word of honour but in his delirium of panic and pain he believed it could remain a secret. There followed a nightmare ride through the storm, his brave white horse galloping madly along lanes running with water, its rider hanging on grimly, near to fainting as blood pumped from his shattered arm.

At length Gaston was in the narrow, sunken lanes of Bramshott. Their banks rose head-high on either side. His horse rushed onwards, flecked with foam, nostrils flaring. Eventually only the river lay between him and Jolliffe's house — the trout river, swollen by hours of heavy rainfall.

A poacher inspecting his traps in the first glimmerings of a rain-sodden dawn saw a rider race across the meadow to put his white horse at the river. It baulked. The rider appeared frantic. A wounded arm hung uselessly. His face was drawn with pain. He wheeled his mount. Again he tried and this time it appeared he would succeed, but the exhausted beast was finished. It landed short, scrabbled pitifully at the slippery far bank for agonising seconds, then fell back into the torrent.

They found horse and rider a mile downstream, wedged in the branches of a fallen willow. Both were quite dead.

The phantom horseman of Bramshott made his first appearance just a few months after that dreadful night. He joined the legion of ghosts that reportedly infest one of England's most haunted villages. Several local worthies scoffed when the first sightings were reported, and put the blame on strong drink or a prankster. They changed their tune when one stout forester, an abstainer to boot, told how

The ghost of a Frenchman on a white horse is said to haunt the sunken lanes of Bramshott.

the apparition had passed straight through his wagon while he cowered and shook with fear.

It is said that on stormy nights over the succeeding years, even well into the 20th century, many terrified individuals have pressed themselves against the high banks of Bramshott's sunken lanes as a ghastly white horse galloped silently past, bearing in its saddle a sightless spectre on a perpetual, hopeless quest to regain his honour. One bloody arm hangs uselessly at his side.

A MATTER OF HONOUR

R arely can an assize judge have been cheered through the streets because his court had acquitted a killer. It happened, though, at Winchester in July of 1846. What made the day even more noteworthy, although neither the judge nor the jubilant crowds could have known it, was that a little piece of history had just been made: the murder trial arose from the last fatal duel ever fought between Englishmen in this country.

The duel took place at Browndown, near Gosport. Such affairs of honour, fought usually between military officers, were by then almost outdated — at least officially. The law was clear and salutary. If a person was killed in a duel, everyone present, whether duellist or second, could be held guilty of murder. Additional sanctions had been threatened against military personnel following the death of an Army colonel during a duel in 1843. Enough was enough, said the War Office. Duelling, proposing a duel, assisting or even failing to prevent one would result in severe punishment under military discipline codes. At the least, an officer could expect to be cashiered.

It was in this knowledge that two men chose an isolated place, well away from prying eyes, to settle their differences with pistols and bullets on the afternoon of 20 May 1845. The whole shambolic affair ended in the unnecessary death of a young ex-Army officer, who it must be said was very much the author of his own misfortune. He simply would not control his lust for Lieutenant Hawkey's wife.

Henry Charles Morehead Hawkey was adjutant of the Royal Marines corps at Portsmouth. It was at an April ball in the city — just one month before the duel — that his wife, 'a woman of great personal attractions', first aroused the attention of James Alexander Seton, who promptly befriended the couple for reasons that soon became abundantly clear. Captain Seton, a married man in his late twenties, had followed no profession since retiring from the 11th Dragoons. This life of ease appears to have suited him well enough, which perhaps accounts for his stout build.

Within days of introducing himself to the Hawkeys, Seton had invited them to dinner at his house. There he shocked Mrs Hawkey by secretly offering her a ring while suggesting 'an improper intimacy'. During the following weeks he became an increasingly frequent visitor to the Hawkeys' lodgings in King's Terrace, generally when the lieutenant was absent at drill or other duties.

His attentions were not welcome. The couple's landlady, a Mrs Stansmore, often heard Mrs Hawkey refer to the corpulent captain as 'that horrible old Seton'. She begged the landlady to tell him that she was not at home if he called, stressing her fear of him. Mrs Hawkey was equally anxious not to let her husband discover the extent of Seton's lechery. She feared the probable consequences.

Seton, though, was incorrigible in his pursuit of the unfortunate woman. One morning he arrived and 'put the proposition to Mrs Hawkey in plain, unambiguous terms'. The following day he again offered the ring and 'spoke of £100 as the purchase of her virtue'. Horrified and hoping to be shot of him, Mrs Hawkey said she would go to her

mother's house near Maidstone. Excellent, replied Seton —
he had a friend near there, where he could stay . . .

She still kept these outrages from her husband, which
must have made matters difficult for her when the couple
frequently joined the Setons at the King's Rooms on
Southsea seafront, near where Clarence Pier stands today.
This smart venue attracted the cream of Portsmouth society
with the best dining, gaming, bathing and dancing in town.
Henry Hollingsworth, joint proprietor of the establishment,
made it his business to know his regular clientele; in his
opinion, the two young men were 'on very friendly terms,
at the rooms together in company almost every day'. But
when Seton danced with Mrs Hawkey, she constantly had
to remind him that his whispered suggestions were
inappropriate from a married man.

Finally suspicious, Hawkey watched the situation with
increasing anxiety. The young lieutenant — he was about
26 — probably hoped matters would resolve themselves. He
was not the sort to look for trouble, at least according to
his fellow officers. At his trial, no fewer than three colonels
'and a great many officers of the Marine corps and other
gentlemen . . . gave [him] the highest character as an officer
and a gentleman, and as a person of a very peaceable and
kind disposition'.

Matters came to a head on 19 May. We don't know what
exactly had occurred but that day Hawkey told Mrs
Stansmore that if Seton called to see his wife she must not
let them be alone for too long, as he had dreadfully insulted
her. Perhaps, he suggested, the landlady could find excuses
to enter the room from time to time, and certainly she should
instantly come to her assistance should Mrs Hawkey ring
the bell. Further evidence of the lieutenant's concern came
in a touching episode later that day, when the landlady
commented on a plant she was tending in the garden. He

replied, 'Mrs Stansmore, bear in mind what I said. Take care of *my* plant — Mrs Hawkey.'

In the event Seton did not arrive. That evening, though, he attended a grand soirée at the King's Rooms where he was seen in the company of the Hawkeys and appeared to be on good terms with them both. Significantly, Mrs Hawkey declined his offer to dance the polka. She did agree to join him in a set of quadrilles, a kind of square dance without close contact, but when he asked her to dance a second set her husband's patience snapped.

Brusquely inviting his erstwhile friend to join him in a nearby card-room, away from the ladies, Hawkey let fly. Seton, he raged, was a blackguard, a scoundrel and a rascal, and unless he gave him 'a meeting' he would horsewhip him up and down the High Street.

According to Seton, when he asked the reason for this outburst Hawkey simply repeated his tirade of abuse and again challenged him. The former dragoon then told the marine that he failed to see why he should risk his life in a duel without knowing the reason. In any case, he added, a light cavalry man could not meet an infantry man. As Hawkey continued to demand satisfaction, Seton left the card-room and soon told a friend, Lieutenant Byron Rowles of the Royal Navy, of his difficulty.

Rowles immediately persuaded a Royal Marines officer at the soirée to intercede with Hawkey in the hope of resolving his grievance amicably that evening — but even he could not placate the irate husband. It was an injury he had received, Hawkey told his brother officer, not merely an insult, and that could not be settled at the King's Rooms. Then he went too far. Did he intend the ultimate provocation? Or was it a further loss of temper that made him aim a kick at Seton's backside as the fat captain passed on his way into the refreshment room? Either way, this public insult was too much. Seton told Hawkey that he now felt compelled to meet him and 'arrangements should be made accordingly'.

Events moved swiftly towards their tragic conclusion. At eight o'clock the following morning, Byron Rowles called at Hawkey's lodgings in his capacity as Seton's second to make arrangements for 'a hostile meeting'. For his part, Hawkey chose as his friend a brother Marines lieutenant, Edward Pym.

These two officers, Rowles and Pym, were later castigated for their part in the affair. Neither had achieved his twentieth birthday. Were they too immature or too excited at the prospect of being involved with a duel to bring the principals to their senses? As Seton lay on his death-bed, the *Hampshire Telegraph* railed against the young officers: 'From this selection of friends, mere boys, resulted, in our estimation, all this mischief; had they possessed the slightest knowledge of the world and the usages of common life, the affair would never have proceeded to a meeting'.

Among the irregularities they permitted, it seems, was that Hawkey himself was allowed to obtain the duelling pistols. His quest that morning took him first to Sherwood's, a gunsmith in Portsmouth High Street, where he tried to borrow a brace of pistols after firing a few test shots with them in the establishment's shooting gallery. After all, he reasoned to himself, he only needed the guns for a single occasion. But Sherwood refused to lend them, so it was off to the premises of Thomas Fiske, also in the High Street. There Hawkey selected a cased pair of duelling pistols with the customary nine-inch barrels and hair triggers, pretending he needed them for a shooting contest he had arranged with Pym. Again a loan was refused, obliging Hawkey to stump up ten guineas to buy the guns.

Now it was back to Sherwood's, this time accompanied

by young Pym, and here an extraordinary event took place. Hawkey practised with his newly purchased duelling pistols on the shooting range before selecting one of the pair with the approving comment, 'That is a damned good pistol!' Then he borrowed a tool from a nearby bench to mark the gun with a small cross.

This was outrageously underhand conduct. Soon after the duel a newspaper reporter somehow heard about Hawkey's practice sessions (but not about the marked pistol). His paper echoed the sentiments of the times when it thundered, 'He ought to be considered as virtually out of the Marine Corps. The man who can practice (*sic*) pistol firing in a public shooting gallery, after having given or accepted a challenge, is no longer fit for the association of gentlemen.'

But that was in the future. For now, Hawkey made his way back home to Southsea, gleefully remarking to Pym, 'I will shoot him like a partridge!' In the middle of the afternoon, Hawkey and Pym took a boat from the sally-port at Portsmouth Point and crossed to Gosport. Pym's 'servant', a marine private, went with them, clutching the pistol case in a brown paper wrapper. The trio walked the remaining few miles to their fateful rendezvous with Seton and Rowles at Browndown.

Set on Gosport's western boundary, the down was ideal for clandestine activity. A long shingle beach bordered acres of scrub and gorse, with here and there a few trees. There was little likelihood of any witnesses at this wild place. Even Pym's servant was barred from the duelling ground, ordered instead to wait on the shore where the shingle bank blocked his view of the action.

The pistols were distributed and loaded — Hawkey doubtless ensuring that the marked favourite came into his hand — then Rowles and Pym withdrew. Their principals now faced each other across a distance of 15 yards. They

presented their weapons. Seton fired first. He missed. Now
it was his turn to stand firm and wait for the other's barrel
to spit its deadly missile. Hawkey took aim, touched the
hair trigger of his pistol — and found it was at half cock.
Perhaps the incompetence of his second was to blame.
Earlier that day, at Sherwood's gallery, young Lieutenant
Pym had been shown for the first time in his life how to
load a duelling piece, and then only once.

At his trial, Hawkey's counsel claimed that under the
duelling code this misfire afforded Seton the opportunity to
display magnanimity and declare honour satisfied, each man
having risked death. Their youthful seconds were criticised,
too, for failing to intervene on the same grounds. But no
such agreement was reached, the guns were reloaded and
Seton fired again. And again he missed.

Hawkey fired almost simultaneously (the police traced a
witness who said he 'heard three shots, one first and then
two together'). Seton must have adopted the classic duelling
position, his right side towards his opponent so as to present
the smallest target. But Seton was a fat man. Hawkey's bullet
struck him in the belly, near his right hip, travelled through
his body and emerged at the left groin.

Needless to say, the inept seconds had not thought to
arrange for any medical assistance to be at hand, so while
Hawkey and Rowles did their best to staunch the blood
pouring from Seton's wounds, Pym ran a mile back to the
beach and returned with his servant, who was then
despatched to fetch a doctor from Gosport.

Hawkey and Pym now decided to make themselves scarce.
First running some three miles to the Fountain Inn, where
they left the pistols wrapped in a sealed parcel to be collected
next day by Pym's servant, they stayed the night at the home
of a Mr Ellis, master of the Queen's yacht *Victoria and
Albert*, without mentioning the duel to him. Next morning

they left and took refuge across the Channel, not to be seen again publicly in this country until their trials a year later.

Meanwhile, two coastguards from the Stokes Bay station had helped Lieutenant Rowles to take Seton out to the yacht *Dream*, which lay in the bay, and there he was given emergency treatment by a surgeon brought from Gosport by Pym's servant. Then the yacht took him the short distance to Old Portsmouth, where he was put to bed at the Quebec Hotel.

Doctors and surgeons from Gosport and Portsmouth visited Seton daily as he lay in some pain but showing hopeful signs of progress, no longer bleeding from his wounds. However, on 27 May, seven days after the duel, they became concerned at indications of internal bleeding from an artery. Finally deciding an operation was essential but beyond their capabilities, they sent to London for the expertise of an eminent surgeon, Mr Liston. On the evening of Saturday 31st, two additional London surgeons helped as Liston cut through abnormal layers of fat to tie off the external iliac artery. 'The operation was a tremendous one,' said one of the surgeons later. 'The deceased was so stout that it was necessary to cut to a great depth to reach the artery.'

All agreed the difficult operation to have been a success. But the patient's condition worsened. On the Monday night, James Alexander Seton died in his bed at the Quebec Hotel. Peritoneal inflammation brought on by the operation was the immediate cause of death, said the medical men.

A coroner's jury trooped from Portsmouth Town Hall to view Seton's body at the Quebec Hotel. Then they heard detailed evidence about events surrounding the duel before deciding that this was a case of wilful murder. The police, who in a short time had already done a commendable job in finding witnesses on both sides of Portsmouth Harbour,

Quebec House in Old Portsmouth, formerly the Quebec Hotel, where Captain Seton died.

redoubled their efforts to bring Hawkey and Pym to account — but to no avail.

The two fugitives remained in hiding until the following February, when their lawyers decided that public outrage over Seton's death had abated sufficiently for them to emerge and face trial. By careful design, Pym surrendered to the police first. He appeared at Winchester Assizes in March 1846, indicted for aiding and abetting Hawkey in the wilful murder of Seton. Mr Serjeant Cockburn fought long and passionately in Pym's defence — his final address to the jury took three hours — but there was no disputing the young officer's guilt and everyone in court awaited the inevitable outcome. Juries, though, have a tradition of returning perverse verdicts. There was utter astonishment all round when they deliberated for just three minutes before finding Pym not guilty.

And there was another surprise. Heartened by the acquittal, Mr Cockburn told the judge that Lieutenant Hawkey was also prepared to surrender if his lordship would hear his case during the present assize. Mr Justice Earle was having none of it. Hawkey should have given himself up sooner, he said. Let the man wait until the next assize.

Hawkey did indeed surrender to his fate, appearing before Mr Baron Platt at Winchester in July 1846 on a very specific indictment. It charged him with the wilful murder of Seton 'by shooting at him with a pistol loaded with a leaden bullet and giving him a mortal wound on the right side'. His months on the run and the prospect of a death sentence were reflected in his appearance. Observers noted that he seemed to have suffered a good deal of anxiety and looked very pale and careworn in the dock.

As the evidence unfolded it became apparent that, as in the case of his friend Pym, there was no disputing Hawkey's guilt. But once again Mr Serjeant Cockburn refused to be deterred, addressing the jury 'in a most eloquent and stirring speech' which lasted two hours. In fact, much of it was a typical lawyer's smokescreen, aimed at confusing the jury while playing on their emotions. His final, outrageous submission was that Hawkey deserved to be acquitted because the indictment had not been proven — Seton died from the effects of the operation, not from the gunshot wound!

The judge delivered a meticulous summation to the jury. Had they heeded his wise words, Hawkey might well have been bound for the scaffold. But if Pym's jury had taken three minutes to return a perverse verdict, these good men and true were determined to beat them. As the judge concluded his address they hesitated barely a second before finding Hawkey not guilty.

Pandemonium broke out. The public benches erupted in approbation, ushers and constables striving in vain to repress the ecstatic crowd. When the hubbub at last subsided, the judge ordered one of the most prominent and noisy demonstrators to be arrested but somehow he managed to escape. 'Nobody seemed disposed to make very violent efforts for his apprehension,' one newspaper reported drily.

Hawkey, the hero of the hour who had shot and killed young Seton, was escorted from the court by back-slapping friends and brother officers. Outside, in the streets of Winchester, the people cheered loudly as he passed and when Mr Baron Platt was driven back to his lodgings they 'saluted his carriage with hearty huzzas'.

So far as is known, this was the last occasion when Englishmen duelled to the death on their native soil. It involved little real honour but a great deal of foolishness.

Perhaps the most astonishing aspect of the whole sordid affair is that Seton genuinely seemed not to understand how his gross conduct had driven Hawkey to extreme measures. Even as the doctors told him to prepare for death, he sobbed and repeated with disbelief what he had always maintained: 'I am perfectly innocent. If I were to die this moment, I know not why I am shot.'

MURDER ON THE COMMON

It was a sad day for Botley when the Tarbert Fencibles arrived to barrack in the village. The columns of raw Irish soldiers came tramping down the rough road from Southampton, red coats dusty in the summer heat, perhaps wishing they had been issued with their muskets and drums so as to make a braver sight as they reached the end of their long journey. Many of them didn't even have uniforms. The regiment numbered 480 at full strength. Ten baggage wagons rumbled into Botley Square, and with them came nearly 500 women and their children.

It was late July in 1799. Soldiers, women and children had travelled — almost entirely on foot — for six months from their homes in the far west of southern Ireland to reach this Hampshire village, where the men were to stand ready to defend England against a French invasion. Along the way, 40 children, 30 women and 13 men were drowned when a lighter capsized in the river Suir before they even left Ireland (some baggage was also lost, which is why many soldiers were now without uniforms). A private soldier had drowned in Gloucestershire, the regiment was searched by a constable for stolen property, an old Salisbury woman complained that soldiers had paid her for gin with counterfeit coins cut from a stolen tin lantern, and every day saw a new crop of desertions. Blistering summer heat forced them to cross

Salisbury Plain at night. Then they had rested for two weeks at Poole and traversed the New Forest before reaching their barracks at Botley, where the regiment was destined to remain for just six months.

These unseasoned troops formed part of the paid Home Guard of their time. Officially, they were His Majesty's Loyal Tarbert Regiment of Fencible Infantry. Most people knew them as the Tarbert Fencibles — a corruption of 'defensibles'.

An Irish baronet, Sir Edward Leslie MP, of Tarbert in County Kerry, had raised the regiment, pursuant to letters of service from George III to provide a defence regiment of infantry for home service in England. Sir Edward's recruiting sergeants toured fairs and markets, banging the drum and enticing gullible country lads with promises of adventure, glory and one pound eight shillings a month. The bribe for joining the Tarberts was a guinea and a meal of beef, bread and beer.

Botley accepted its Irish guests with the same ambivalence it had displayed towards their Welsh predecessors, the Carmarthenshire Militia (who, in a move that presumably made sense to the military mind, now marched away for service in Ireland), and towards all the other troops who had been stationed there throughout the 18th century. The arrival of the Fencibles meant good business for tradespeople and publicans — for example, the reward for quartering a soldier was a halfpenny a day — but at the same time the influx of a thousand or more souls inevitably had implications for a rural community numbering just 614. Petty theft, poaching, brawling and similar minor disruptions were commonplace, despite the regiment's efforts to keep its troops and their families in order.

Some respite came in late August, when the Army district commander decided that there were too many women with the regiment. He ordered most of them back to Ireland. Some 400 women and their children walked from Botley to Bristol, sailed to Cork and then walked the width of southern Ireland to the homes they had left in February. Their subsistence and fares cost the regiment £505.

September arrived, and with it a wagon bringing the regiment's long-awaited weapons and drums from the armoury at the Tower of London. Among these arms were 600 flintlock muskets for issue to the private soldiers. They were the common 'India pattern' guns originally designed for the East India Company's private army but for emergency reasons adopted as the regular army's regulation musket. Each gun came with a formidable bayonet, its 17-inch triangular blade measuring one and a quarter inches at the base.

The people of Botley were destined to hear much about that wicked bayonet. For now, though, life in the village and within the regiment proceeded without undue incident. The troops were instructed in the use of their new weapons. They went on manoeuvres, got drunk, cared for their families, stole poultry, game and winter vegetables for the pot, received new uniforms to replace those lost in the river tragedy and fraternised with the locals. One of the regiment's women, Catherine Brown, soon persuaded a Botley man into marriage, while Private Thomas Connor married Ann Hilman, also from Botley parish. The colonel was pleased to note that only five soldiers deserted during the winter; a few made it back to Ireland, only to surrender themselves and return to Botley with loss of pay their only punishment.

The awful event that has imprinted the memory of the Tarbert Fencibles indelibly into Botley's history took place on Tuesday, 11 February 1800. That evening, Mr Daniel Barfoot was going about his business at his home, which stood at the far end of Outlands Lane, about a mile away from Botley across Curdridge Common. The remains of what is believed to have been Barfoot's tiny red-brick cottage are still there, in the grounds of The Cedars.

Which of the Barfoot family first noticed him is not known, but staggering and crawling across the rough common and up to the sanctuary of their door came a pitiful sight. Half conscious, in intense pain and covered with dirt, blood and wounds, the old man appeared close to death as the Barfoots helped him into their cottage. That he was alive at all was a miracle — they were horrified to see, rammed into his neck and head, the broken stump of an army bayonet, six and a half inches in length.

Thomas Webb was at least 70 years old and lived in impoverished conditions at Swanmore, from where, according to some sources, he would walk from village to village peddling a few pathetic items of woodenware. It beggars belief that his assailants could have mistaken this poor, shabby old pedlar for a rich farmer, but so the story goes. Leaving a shop in Botley after buying six eggs, Webb made his way out of the village, followed by two soldiers with villainy on their minds. On the edge of Curdridge Common, near the spot known as Pinkmead Corner, they set about him 'in the most inhuman manner'.

The wretched old man was stabbed and cut in various parts of the head and body. Then the soldiers dragged him over an adjoining bank, threw him into a ditch and stamped upon him with their heavy army boots. The thugs made off with his eggs and the small amount of money he had on his person — a few shillings, according to some contemporary accounts; others say it was as little as seven pence.

Despite his grievous injuries, Thomas Webb dragged himself from the ditch and somehow made his way across the common for nearly a mile to Barfoot's cottage. They sent for a surgeon who removed the bayonet and generally did his best, but without much hope. Webb gasped out his horrific tale, as a result of which Daniel Barfoot and his son at once loaded their guns and bravely went in search of the soldiers. They didn't find them but word was sent to the officers of the Tarbert Fencibles that their men were suspected of robbery with extreme violence that evening. The bloody bayonet also went to the barracks.

Captain Godfrey Massey arrived at the barracks at nine o'clock and ordered an immediate roll-call. Everyone was present. They thought they had their man when the shoemaker's bayonet was found to be missing, so the unfortunate soldier was locked up until enquiries confirmed that he had been in his room all day.

The captain meanwhile set about establishing which of his men had been out that evening. A group were found to have returned to barracks from the canteen shortly before the snap roll-call, one of whom, a Private John Diggon, had had something concealed under his coat. Could this have been a broken bayonet? Or was it six eggs, stolen from a poor old man? Captain Massey's enquiries resulted in the arrest of Diggon, Private Richard Prendergast and Sergeant James Collopy on suspicion of complicity in the crime. These three were taken before a magistrate. He committed them in custody for further examination by the coroner, for by now Thomas Webb had died.

Exciting events took place on the following Saturday. The people of Botley turned out to watch the Tarbert Fencibles march from their village, never to return. The regiment had been transferred to barracks at Winchester, possibly as a routine posting or perhaps in deference to the Webb incident.

Also that Saturday, Mr Green, the coroner, opened his inquest at the place on the common where old Thomas

Webb had been attacked. The hearing resumed at 11 o'clock on Monday morning at the Dolphin in Botley Square, when clearly the jury were given much to occupy their minds, for it was not until midnight that they brought in a verdict of wilful murder against the three soldiers. Mr Green promptly committed them for trial at the next assizes.

On 4 March, at the Lent Assizes held at Winchester Castle, no bill of indictment was preferred against Sergeant Collopy. Private Prendergast was tried and acquitted on grounds of insufficient evidence. Diggon alone was convicted of the murder and sentenced to death, protesting his innocence. However, when two of his officers and the under sheriff went to tell him to prepare himself for execution, they found Diggon praying God's forgiveness.

He then told them that when he and Prendergast had overtaken Thomas Webb, it was Prendergast who stopped the old man, took the bayonet from Diggon's belt and administered all the wounds before robbing him. The only part he, Diggon, had played was to take Webb's feet and help Prendergast throw him into the ditch.

Prendergast, of course, had been found not guilty by the criminal court. But the Army still made him suffer. Ostensibly for disobedience to orders, a court martial sentenced him to 1,000 lashes and to be drummed out of the regiment with a rope around his neck. Incredibly, after receiving the first 600 strokes on 14 March 'he did not seem to be the least affected,' according to one observer. The remaining 400 lashes were administered at a later date.

John Diggon was already dead. He went to the gallows near Winchester on 10 March, first clearing his conscience by publicly confessing to another robbery near Botley, when he had stolen a piece of gold, some silver and a key from a middle-aged man. He begged pardon of this victim and of Thomas Webb's widow and friends. Diggon prayed fervently, declaring that he preferred instant death to a longer life under the burden of his crimes. Then they hanged him.

In accordance with his sentence, the next day his body was taken to Botley and suspended in chains on a gibbet at Curdridge Common, near the spot where the murder had been committed. It was the usual punishment for highway robbery, intended to act as a grisly warning to others. Gibbets Corner, alongside a stream behind The End in Outlands Lane, was recorded in the Ordnance Survey of 1810, as was an engraved memorial stone perpetuating the murder. Its wording (complete with spelling errors) was later transferred to a cast-iron plate which, after several moves, now rests near Botley railway station.

A cast-iron plate near Botley railway station commemorates 'a most cruel murder'.

It is said that Diggon's remains hung in the chains for 40 years before the common warden, old Master Hickley, buried the bones in his garden in Outlands Lane.

The Tarbert Fencibles were never required to fight an enemy. The regiment was disbanded in 1802 but not before another of their number had been sentenced to death for murder. In reality they were probably no better nor worse than other military units of their day. Soon after Thomas Webb's murder, all non-commissioned officers, drummers and privates voluntarily donated half a day's pay to help his widow and family, while expressing 'a full determination always to prove ourselves good soldiers and peaceable citizens'.

THE CALSHOT S5 MYSTERY

Under other circumstances it might have been a pleasant afternoon on the Solent. The wintry weather of recent days had given way to a welcome March sun, with hardly a breath of wind to ruffle the surface of the sea. But none of this could lift the air of melancholy in the boats and among the watchers on the shore at Calshot.

It was Tuesday, 13 March 1928. At around noon the diving ship *Excellent* had arrived from Portsmouth naval yard to drop anchor at the mouth of Southampton Water, not far from Castle Point buoy. Her three divers now sat patiently on a small launch, waiting in their cumbersome suits as two crews in rowing boats methodically dragged the seabed with chains. They had been at it for most of the afternoon. The water here was among the deepest in the Solent and great ocean steamers thrashed along the fairway out of Southampton, each one dipping its ensign in salutation to a dead hero as it passed the searchers and realised the grim task on which they were engaged.

They dragged and dived for four hours before locating the wreckage of the tiny seaplane. It was just a few hundred yards from the spot where it had plunged into the sea some 24 hours previously. The pilot's body still sat in the open cockpit. Among other terrible injuries, he had been decapitated.

First they raised its engine, which had broken away from the fuselage. Then the fuselage itself and the tail of the machine were brought to the surface, secured to a trawler and towed slowly down the Solent to Calshot Aerodrome, where the headless body was extricated and taken off in an ambulance. Awaiting the wreckage was Major James Cooper, an Inspector of Accidents, who had been appointed by the Secretary of State for Air to investigate the mysterious death of one of the world's greatest airmen.

At a time of intense interest in the science of aviation, when nations competed to see whose aircraft could be fastest and best, the name of Flight-Lieutenant Samuel 'Kink' Kinkead was guaranteed to stir British hearts. He had become a national hero even before his attempt on the world air speed record, an ace pilot whose real-life exploits during and after the First World War read like a *Boy's Own* adventure.

Kinkead's illustrious flying career began at the age of 18, when he volunteered as a probationary sub-lieutenant with the Royal Naval Air Service in September 1915. The following year, his pilot's training completed, Kinkead flew in the Dardanelles campaign, where he scored his first three aerial 'kills'. September 1917 saw him promoted to flight-lieutenant and in action over the hellish front line of the Somme. Within two months he destroyed six German aircraft. Soon his skill and determination in attacking enemy machines were being hailed as an inspiration to other pilots. Once, having just shot down a hostile plane, he was seen to single-handedly engage and drive off a group of seven others. Transferred to the Ypres front towards the end of 1917, his Sopwith Camel soon claimed a further five 'kills', and his conspicuous gallantry in aerial combat was recognised with the award of the Distinguished Service Cross.

An S5 seaplane, similar to the one in which Flt. Lt. Kinkead was killed near Calshot. (Fawley Historians)

In April 1918, when the RNAS merged with the Royal Flying Corps to become the RAF, his naval squadron became 201 Squadron. By the end of the war Kinkead was 201's highest scoring airman, credited with a total of 33 'kills'. Besides a Bar to his DSC, he also held the Distinguished Flying Cross and Bar. He was not yet 22 years of age. Examples of his courage and daring included the notable occasion when he repeatedly flew his flimsy Camel against gunfire in order to dislodge a large party of enemy troops from a wood, at the same time fighting off the attentions of six hostile fighter planes. The engagement lasted an hour but his persistent bravery was rewarded when the soldiers broke and ran, and later he rounded off his day by shooting down an enemy two-seater which was harassing the British line.

After the war Kinkead served in Russia with the Allied

Intervention Force, claiming ten 'kills' of Red Russian aircraft. Again he earned the highest praise for successful attacks at considerable personal risk against troops, artillery, camps and transport. In October 1919, when 5,000 Red Army cavalry broke through and threatened to jeopardise the defence of Tzaritzin, it was Kinkead who led four Sopwith Camels in a series of hair-raising low-level attacks that dispersed the enemy, killing more than 1,600 and saving the day. That action earned him the Distinguished Service Order.

Into the 1920s, and Flt. Lt. Kinkead is an instructor at Cranwell before joining 30 Squadron in Iraq. The man's daring exploits continued: risking death from hostile gunfire, he and another pilot landed their aircraft, rescued the crew of a crashed RAF plane and took off again under a hail of bullets.

This was precisely the calibre of cool, skilful and committed young men sought by the RAF for its High Speed Flight. Just three pilots were selected, all flight-lieutenants, and 1927 saw them based for two months at RAF Calshot, the flying boat base on the New Forest shore of the Solent, practising in preparation for that year's Schneider Trophy contest. Their hopes were pinned on the Supermarine S5, a single-seat racing seaplane, designed through the genius of R.J. Mitchell, powered by a mighty 875 hp Napier Lion engine and built by Supermarine Aviation at Southampton. From the S5 and its successors emerged Mitchell's most famous achievement — the Spitfire.

Flt. Lt. Webster flew the winning circuit at Venice that year, reaching almost 282 mph in the S5 to regain the Schneider Trophy for Britain. Kinkead's own brilliant performance attracted considerable praise, and in the light of what was to happen to him the following year it is timely to consider this admiring account of his flying prowess at

Kinkead (second from right) with other members of the RAF High Speed Flight. (Fawley Historians)

Venice: 'So evenly did he make the turns and so exactly did he maintain his height of a few feet from the water, that it appeared as if his machine were running on rails.'

This, then, was the situation of Sam Kinkead in 1928, the year after Venice. At the age of 31 he was fêted by his country, acknowledged as a superb pilot, a member of an incredibly élite team which had beaten the best the world could offer. He enjoyed an exemplary record of success and bravery in several theatres of war. And he shared other attributes with Biggles, that quintessentially British fictional airman — he, too, was an unassuming, clean-living, thoroughly decent chap. One of his contemporaries spoke of Kinkead as 'thinking straight, talking straight and living straight'. Another referred to him as 'straight as a die in all his dealings with his juniors and seniors . . . modest in the extreme . . . a tremendous personality'. With Kinkead's death, added this former fighter ace, 'the RAF lost, without doubt, its finest junior officer'.

The High Speed Flight returned to Calshot in February 1928. Their mission was to snatch the world air speed record from Italy. The pilot chosen for the attempt was Kinkead. His Supermarine S5 had been built for the 1927 Schneider contest, taken to Venice as a reserve plane and later modified, brought to a peak of perfection by the experts from Supermarine and Napier.

By early March, when the attempt was due to be made, the world's press were entrenched at Calshot. Five frustrating days waiting mainly for the weather to improve were rewarded on Sunday, 11 March when Kinkead took the S5 on a 17-minute test flight. It was a riveting performance, the tiny blue and silver monoplane screaming across the Solent towards the Isle of Wight, then climbing almost vertically to make its turns before swooping low and returning for high speed runs along the waterway off Calshot, sometimes at a height of barely 100 feet. Wedged in its open cockpit, inadequately protected against the icy cold by RAF trousers, a Fair Isle sweater, flying helmet and goggles, Kinkead impressed observers with the 'superb manner' in which he handled the plane. 'His magnificent control of high speed aircraft is almost superhuman,' enthused one reporter, while his landing on the water at the end of the trial 'was a masterpiece of skill and neat calculation.

Air Force pilots, who were among the onlookers on the Air Station, were unanimous that it was the neatest piece of alighting they had ever witnessed.' Mark those words.

At six the following morning, Kinkead watched as Napier's engineer began tuning the engine in preparation for an official attempt on the world speed record. Suddenly its oil cooler sprang a leak due to the oil thickening in the extreme cold, as a result of which the cooler was rushed up-river for repair at the Supermarine works in Woolston and replaced on the S5 by early afternoon.

A blinding snowstorm raged for most of the afternoon, causing more anxiety. Right up until 4.30, Kinkead and others had doubts as to whether an attempt would be possible. Then the arrival of brilliant sunshine provided a window of opportunity and the S5 was run down the slipway into flat-calm water. Despite the intense cold, Kinkead stripped to the same clothing as previously before climbing into the narrow, open cockpit. He had difficulty taking off, an operation requiring a speed of about 100 mph, but after ten minutes the plane left the water on his second attempt and shot into the air like a bullet.

To comply with Federation Aeronatique Internationale regulations, the S5 had to complete another test flight before attempting the speed record, so Kinkead soon reappeared from the direction of Cowes, made a perfect landing on the water and immediately took off again. That was his test flight. Now for the record.

At about 5.25 the crowds on the jetties, the foreshore, the slipways and the roof of Calshot Castle strained their eyes towards the Isle of Wight as a tiny silver speck hurtled towards them, rapidly increasing in size. Estimated to be travelling at between 200 and 300 mph, Kinkead deliberately lost height to about 250 feet as he approached the measured three kilometre course. This was it. The excited onlookers had no doubts — Kinkead was coming in for the first lap in an attempt to smash the air speed record.

The disaster was sudden, spectacular and horrifying. One moment the beautiful little seaplane was streaking past Calshot, its height now somewhere between 50 and 100 feet above the water, Kinkead seeming to open the throttle even wider — and then it abruptly nosedived, almost vertically, its heavy engine dragging it down below the surface, to be lost from sight in an instant. A shower of spray soon subsided. Then there was nothing.

Sam Kinkead was buried with full military honours at All Saints' church in Fawley four days after the accident. It required three RAF lorries to carry the floral tributes. An inquest had opened the previous day, endeavouring to discover how the tragedy could possibly have arisen. The S5 was a supreme piece of design, expertly built and maintained. So was its engine. Its pilot ranked among the world's finest. What could have gone wrong?

There was no shortage of theories. Many of them centred on that open cockpit which exposed the pilot not only to the biting cold but also to the danger of inhaling fumes from the fuel supply and the engine's open exhaust. Kinkead was visibly affected by the cold after the previous day's test run. Did he somehow freeze up? Had his goggles or windshield iced over? Did the intense cold cause an engine malfunction?

The team's engineers were convinced of the absolute integrity of both aircraft and engine, and there can be no doubting their sincerity in saying they would not have allowed the attempt to proceed otherwise. But did something go wrong later, during the difficult take-off perhaps? Had the tail or some other vital part been weakened by the strain? It seems not. Major Cooper, the government's Inspector of Accidents, reported that no part of the structure, controls or engine had broken or failed to function normally.

Attention focused on the fact that Kinkead had previously

complained of being upset by fumes. He felt unwell during the Schneider Trophy flights and had brought back his breakfast after Sunday's test flight of the S5. The coroner seemed fixated with the question of fumes, asking repeated — but fruitless — questions about the composition of the plane's unique fuel mixture, which included tetraethyl of lead. Witnesses were reluctant to reveal its formula, even quoting the Official Secrets Act.

Was Kinkead overcome by fumes? It came almost as a disappointment to the coroner when, at the resumed inquest 11 days later, a report from the RAF Pathological Laboratory revealed no evidence of poison by exhaust or petrol fumes in Kinkead's body. Death, said the pathologist, was due to the accident impact.

Fuelling the S5 at Calshot. Did fumes overcome Sam Kinkead on his record-breaking attempt? (Fawley Historians)

The official cause of the crash came eventually from Major Cooper. There was absolutely nothing wrong with the S5, he claimed, and Kinkead's sickness after the Sunday test probably resulted from eating breakfast on a cold and empty stomach, not from inhaling fumes. In his opinion Kinkead had decided to abandon the record attempt because of weather conditions. In attempting to land he had misjudged his height, had lost sufficient speed to maintain flight and the S5 had stalled. It was a common cause of accidents, he said, adding that under such weather conditions, with mistiness, little wind and a calm sea, it was difficult to judge height over water.

And that was that. Human error. Cooper had decided that a man renowned for his daring low-level flying throughout his service career, particularly while piloting the fastest aircraft in the world, admired for his skill at landing on water and who had made a perfect landing just minutes before the crash, suddenly got it fatally wrong.

Was there an official cover-up? Considerable national prestige rode on the S5. It is probable, too, that there were military implications behind its development and design. And its fuel was clearly a secret. Only a military man — Cooper — inspected the wreckage. Only an RAF pathologist inspected Kinkead's remains. The S5 and the RAF were declared blameless. It was entirely the pilot's fault. Why, though, did the coroner initially press witnesses so strongly on the question of fumes? What had he heard about Kinkead's death?

RAF Calshot is now Calshot Activities Centre. Its main conference room was named after Flt. Lt. Kinkead during memorial events held in 1998 to commemorate the 70th anniversary of a brave pilot's death. It overlooks the scene of a terrible accident whose cause, despite the official verdict, remains shrouded in mystery.

THE THREE LYONS MURDER

Was it simply the sight of his plump saddle-bags that marked the traveller for murder? Or did his killer actually hear the tempting chink of heavy gold coins and gamble that the reward would be worth the risk? Whatever the case, Joseph Tracy rode into Fordingbridge on horseback, entered the Three Lyons on foot and left horizontally in a wooden casket, stabbed and robbed and quite dead. The year was 1684 and folk said the town had never known a more dreadful business.

They also wondered how Sam could have done such a thing. It was Sam, ostler at the Three Lyons for many a year, who had left the inn's cosy fireside, tipsy and grumbling, to brave the bitter November night as Mr Tracy's horse clattered into the yard. Sam it was who carried his heavy saddle-bags into the inn. They found the bloody, damning evidence in Sam's possession and it was Sam who now shivered in a Winchester dungeon, awaiting execution for the murder.

By a cruel irony, Tracy would have lived had the weather not forced him to abandon the idea of reaching Ringwood that night. The Three Lyons in Fordingbridge High Street offered a welcome refuge after his hard ride from Shaftesbury across Cranborne Chase, and it was a thoroughly exhausted traveller who staggered upstairs to bed at one o'clock with his belly full of supper and wine, saddle-bags over one shoulder. Accordingly, Martha Moore, the chambermaid, was not surprised when he failed to answer her repeated knockings on his door at seven the next morning. But her impatience became concern upon finding she could not open the door.

Stupid Sam was no help when he passed, hung-over and bleary-eyed as usual. 'Perhaps he's been murdered,' he grunted. 'How could he be?' asked Martha, indicating the locked door. 'There's other ways than doors into people's rooms,' said the dullard cryptically, and clumped off towards the stables in his heavy boots. Ultimately it was the landlord, Mr Porter, who put his shoulder to the locked door and discovered the traveller lying in a large pool of blood on the floor, partly dressed and barely alive. Attempted suicide, declared Porter, before sending Martha running for the doctor.

Tracy lived just long enough to gasp some of his story to Dr Highmore. He had not tried to take his own life. After locking the door he had fallen on the bed, half undressed, tired and dizzy. The sound of money brought him to his senses and to his feet, remembering the large amount of gold coins and bank notes in his saddle-bags. Someone seized him from behind. He was stabbed during the ensuing brief struggle, but not before noticing in the moonlight that his assailant resembled the . . . And at that point, without waiting to identify the killer, Tracy inconveniently died.

His rifled saddle-bags confirmed the motive for murder — but how had the killer got into his room? The question vexed Magistrate Bulkeley and the constable of the Hundred as they examined the scene. The windows were secure and the key, albeit slightly bloodstained, was still in the inside lock.

When Martha, with some hesitation, repeated what Sam

had said not an hour before, suspicion at once fell on the slow-witted ostler. Was he the murderer so nearly identified in Tracy's dying words? The constable went off to search Sam's room, found three bloodstained bank notes concealed in his bedside slippers and promptly took him before the magistrate. Sam could not — or would not — account for either the money or his movements, claiming to have slept all night in a drunken stupor. He must have got in through Tracy's window somehow, decided the magistrate, and with no one to support his alibi the circumstantial evidence was sufficient to see the ostler quickly tried at Winchester, convicted of murder and sentenced to hang.

There the matter would have rested had not Martha Moore and her lover been convinced of Sam's innocence. The lover's brother, John Pearce, was a government secret agent in London, a man who thrived on mystery and so responded positively to their letter entreating his help. Taking the earliest possible coach to Hampshire, he called first at Winchester Castle, where he used his influence to persuade the governor to defer Sam's execution. Then another coach took him across the flat New Forest plain to Fordingbridge and the Three Lyons. His identity and mission he kept secret.

Landlord Porter had no reason to doubt Pearce's cover story. His welcome for 'Mr Hunter' was effusive. Certainly he had room at his inn for a gentleman from London, and he hoped he would enjoy his holiday, even though the gentleman had heard about the recent unpleasantness and 'wished to indulge his interest in ghosts' by occupying the late Mr Tracy's room. What Porter did not witness was Pearce's clandestine meeting with Martha and her lover, when he questioned them closely about what had transpired.

His examination of the murder scene quickly satisfied Pearce that the leaded window panes had never been

The ancient bridge over the Avon brought John Pearce into Fordingbridge to unmask a killer.

disturbed. The only other way into the room was by the door, which of course Tracy had locked upon retiring, leaving the key on the inside. So how did the killer get in? Pearce lay in the murdered man's room, kept from sleep by the mystery — until suddenly he imagined he heard a noise from under his bed. Of course! The murderer had not broken in at all. He was already there, concealed in the room, when Tracy arrived. But how had he managed to leave the key on the inside as he escaped? Pearce pondered far into the night. He already had a suspect in mind.

In the ensuing days, landlord Porter found 'Mr Hunter' a most engaging and entertaining fellow. In fact, so taken was he with his guest that he hesitated only briefly before agreeing to lend 'Hunter' £200 at interest, in the belief that he needed to quickly clinch a property deal. Disappointingly for the sleuth, Porter produced the cash in gold coin rather than in notes which he might have compared with those found in Sam's slippers.

Within hours Pearce was outlining his suspicions to the governor at Winchester. Sam's claim to have been dead drunk was probably true, he said. In that drunken condition, Martha had confirmed, the ostler would lie stupefied on his bed all night, fully clothed, right down to the big boots she had seen him wearing on the fateful morning. But on the rare occasions when Sam was sufficiently sober to undress before retiring, he invariably wore slippers, not boots, until nine or ten o'clock the following morning. A drunken man could not have committed the crime — and anyway, those clumping boots would have betrayed him in the night. Furthermore, why were only three notes found in his room? The man was far from bright. Surely the rest of the cash would have been there?

The bloodstained notes indicated that the killer had Tracy's blood on his hands, Pearce continued. There was also blood on the key — but nowhere else on the door. Who would have been sufficiently familiar with the room to reach straight for the key in the darkness? Certainly not an ostler.

Pearce now produced the £200 loaned by Porter. There was no blood on the gold coins but they were in a cash bag made of ticking, which appeared to have been washed thoroughly. Why should anyone bother to wash a money bag? To remove bloodstains, perhaps. Was it possible that Tracy's employers, Perkins and Radley, could identify it as one of theirs? The governor agreed to contact them.

And so it proved. Not only was it similar to their bags, the thread used to make the ticking was unknown in the Fordingbridge area. Back at the Three Lyons, the constable joined John Pearce in searching Porter's room under a magistrate's warrant. Pearce's experience led him unerringly to an old bureau. As he had anticipated, careful examination revealed one small drawer to be slightly shorter than the others, which in turn resulted in the discovery of a secret compartment behind it. Inside were bank notes consecutive with those already found, together with the bloodstained murder weapon — an oyster knife.

Porter confessed. He had indeed hidden under Tracy's bed, awaiting his arrival with the saddle-bags, meaning only to rob him as he slept, but in the unintended struggle the oyster knife — a tool of his trade — came to hand and he struck out. Porter instinctively locked the door as he left, taking the key with him. The idea then came to him of disposing of the only three bloodstained notes by planting them on poor Sam, who lay snoring drunk in his bed. Sam could take the blame for the crime. Finally, Porter had replaced the key inside Tracy's room while Martha was fetching Dr Highmore. He could not explain why he had concealed the knife, other than that he could not bear to see it.

So the landlord went to the gallows, his inn was converted into a private house and Sam returned home in triumph, vowing never to touch another drop of drink. But was there really a murder at the Three Lyons in 1684?

This tale came to light many years ago in an old leather-bound volume bought at a book sale, its publication date unrecorded. Written inside was 'Jeremiah Cray, Ibbesley, 1790, His Booke'. It provides no clues to the intriguing question: Is the Three Lyons murder mystery a true story — or merely a piece of 18th century detective fiction?

DEATH OF A MERRY WIDOW

Alice Mary Carhart deserved a better death. She was one of those fun-loving ladies who enjoy nothing better than a lively evening with friends at the pub. A little over five feet tall, slimly built and bespectacled, the 67-year-old widow was a popular figure in her local, the Waggon and Horses, which stood close to her home in the Brooks area of Winchester. That was where she spent a happy Friday evening in early December 1963, laughing, drinking, smoking, and perhaps trying to forget the approach of a fifth Christmas without her late husband. Their only daughter had died ten years previously, so now the widow lived quite alone in her terraced house in Lower Brook Street. The ground floor used to be the Carharts' small general store. She had closed the business soon after her husband died but she kept herself active with a little job as tea lady at the nearby factory of Kennett's Price Markers. Alice was Fanny or Fan to most of her friends. Sometimes, to her delight, they called her the Merry Widow.

Alice lived up to her reputation that Friday evening at the Waggon and Horses. She passed a very pleasant evening among friends. After closing time there followed what publicans euphemistically refer to as 'a private party in the back room'. Drink and good humour flowed freely behind locked doors. Alice enjoyed herself immensely but when she began spilling her whisky, somewhere around midnight, her friends wisely decided that it was time for bed. Two of them escorted her home. She had been nervous since suffering a burglary two weeks previously, so before returning to the party the men checked the house, said goodnight to her in the hallway and made sure she had bolted the front door behind them. The time was about 12.15 am. Alice would be dead within three hours.

It was nearly mid-morning before her workmates at Kennett's, missing their cups of tea, became concerned at her absence from work. They tried knocking on her door. Then they enquired at the Waggon and Horses, and ultimately it was a fireman, summoned from the nearby North Walls fire station by the pub landlady, who climbed a ladder to the open window of her first-floor bedroom and discovered the body.

She lay at an angle on one of two single beds, eyes open, nearly naked, two vests and a slip pushed up under her arms. Strewn around lay other torn underclothes. There were signs of a minor scuffle in the room, causing police investigators to consider the possibility that Alice, a diabetic, had thrashed about while suffering a fatal fit. Not until much later in the day did a post-mortem examination confirm their true suspicions. Somewhere between 12.30 and 3 in the morning, said the pathologist, Mrs Carhart had suffered 'death by mechanical asphyxiation'. In lay terms, she had been suffocated by having a pillow held over her face. She had also been sexually assaulted.

Within hours of Fireman Cox's grim discovery, CID chiefs had launched a full-scale murder investigation. Detectives drawn from police stations throughout the county were called from their homes, their weekend leave cancelled, to make their way to Winchester. There they were formed into teams and given precise lines of enquiry, following a well-tried plan which had earned the Hampshire force an enviable reputation in murder investigation. This case proved to be almost a textbook enquiry. The clues unearthed by the detective officers were followed up swiftly, leading to an arrest within 24 hours.

The investigators soon established that an unsuccessful attempt had been made to force Mrs Carhart's front door with a steel bar which they found nearby in the gutter. Refusing to be thwarted, her killer had then climbed a drainpipe, forced his way in through the bedroom window, ripped off her clothing during a violent sexual assault, suffocated her and then left through the bedroom door, locking it and taking the key. The house had not been ransacked and it appeared that no valuables had been stolen. Even the few pounds in Alice's handbag were untouched.

There seemed little doubt that the intruder had one thing in mind when he undertook his determined assault on the house. And it was a fair presumption that he was someone who knew the Merry Widow would be alone and helpless in her bed.

Scenes of crime officers now began a painstaking search, examining every inch of the house for the most minute clues. Their colleagues meanwhile were knocking on every door in and around Lower Brook Street, questioning all the residents, while others were detailed to find everyone who had been at the Waggon and Horses the previous night.

Two strangers soon popped into the frame. They were at the pub party until shortly before midnight. One of them, a young Scotsman, had paid a lot of attention to Mrs Carhart, at one stage sitting with his arm around her shoulders. None of the regulars at the Waggon and Horses knew them. So who were these men? What light could they throw on the enquiry? Most important of all, where did they go after the party? Detectives worked into the cold

December night, tracing and questioning every taxi driver who had been on duty in Winchester the previous evening — and came up trumps.

A driver working from the taxi rank in the Broadway remembered two men who answered the descriptions. They had come to the rank soon after midnight and he had dropped one of them at a house in Wharf Hill before running the other, a Scotsman, to an address in Fivefields Road, which the Scot said was his lodgings. During the journey the garrulous young man wouldn't stop talking. He claimed to have been drinking since six o'clock, ending the evening in the company of a woman with whom he might have spent the night, had his friend not cramped his style. To cap it all, he complained, two other men had taken her home.

Here was a promising lead. These were obviously the men from the pub. But the taxi driver then volunteered some additional information that really caused the interviewing detective to sit up and take notice. In the very early hours of the morning, returning from another trip to the outskirts of Winchester, he had been surprised to pass someone who appeared to be the Scotsman he had taken home not long previously. Surprised, because the young man was now walking back towards the city centre — in which direction lay Lower Brook Street.

With the assistance of the taxi driver, the police soon traced his fares. The man from Wharf Hill explained how he had spent the Friday evening drinking in several pubs with a Scottish friend, Willy MacDonald. He confirmed that they were the men who had been in the Waggon and Horses. At the after-hours party, Willy had been chatting and drinking with an older woman they called Fanny, with whom he seemed to be on fairly friendly terms, but two of the regulars took her home. He and Willy had then walked to the Broadway to find a taxi and once at home he had gone straight to bed. Police soon cleared this man of suspicion, although they exchanged knowing glances when he later made a comment on his friend's astonishing climbing prowess. Apparently he had once seen Willy shin swiftly up a chain that hung through two storeys of a grain store. A widow's drainpipe would pose no challenge to such an athlete.

William Jackson MacDonald, a 23-year-old labourer with the local water board, was roused from sleep at his lodgings in Fivefields Road at 9.45 on the Sunday morning. Detective Sergeant Arthur Bevis had been detailed to bring him in for interview. He looked at MacDonald with the shrewd eye of experience. Could this be their man? After readily agreeing that he had been at the pub in the company of Alice Carhart on the Friday evening, MacDonald went with the detectives to the police station where he made a formal statement about his movements. It was the same story as his friend's. MacDonald, though, added that he already had a slight acquaintance with Alice, as he had met her while working on the water supply for a new health clinic near her home in Lower Brook Street. He thought she was about 60. He had spoken to her at the pub party, had bought her a drink and at one stage put his arms round her. She had not objected. As the party drew to a close, he asked her if she was going to take him home for coffee but she said she couldn't. He had definitely seen nothing more of her after she left the pub with her friends.

When the taxi delivered him to his lodgings that night, MacDonald continued, he awakened his landlady for permission to make a cup of coffee in her kitchen. She agreed but he found the gas had run out. Then he had slept for a while on a chair in the kitchen before rousing himself and going straight to bed, where he stayed until late on the

A PC guards the murder scene. Police used the ladder to remove a drainpipe for examination. (Bob Sollars, Winchester)

Saturday morning, sleeping off the effects of ten or more pints of beer.

Although his landlady corroborated his alibi as regards waking her in the night, the police were far from happy with Willy MacDonald. He was going nowhere for a while. As the interviewing officers took him through his story again and again, his room was being searched thoroughly. All his possessions were carefully bagged and brought in for inspection. Among them were a cigarette holder, a part-used packet of Richmond cigarettes and a clock key. Small, apparently insignificant objects in normal circumstances, they were to become vital evidence in the murder enquiry.

The police had noticed that MacDonald rolled his own cigarettes. Why should he have a packet of Richmond and a cigarette holder? Alice Carhart was a habitual smoker but Richmond was not her preferred brand, said the landlady of the Waggon and Horses. And then she remembered something that began to make the jigsaw pieces fall into place.

On the Thursday evening Alice had won a little prize in the pub's darts team raffle. It was a packet of 20 cigarettes. She had passed them round a few friends before putting the remainder in her pocket. The landlady even remembered the brand. It was Richmond.

Had MacDonald now said Alice had given him the cigarettes at the pub on the Friday evening, it might have closed a promising line of enquiry. So the officers posed the question carefully: Where did he get that packet of Richmonds? From a vending machine somewhere in Winchester, he replied, a claim that saw detectives despatched to make enquiries at every cigarette outlet in the city. No machine dispensed such packets, they reported back. MacDonald's explanation had to be false.

The pub landlady and several of her regulars were shown the cigarette holder. They identified it as belonging to the Merry Widow. So, too, did the little key which close friends had often seen Alice use to wind the clock on her mantelpiece.

MacDonald was questioned about bloodstains found on his clothes. He claimed they could have been caused during a fight outside a pub the previous month, while a slight accident at work probably accounted for blood on his shirt.

There was an air of optimism at murder headquarters as the evidence continued to stack up, but in the face of his denials they had yet to prove that their suspect had been anywhere near Mrs Carhart's house on the night she was killed. Now another line of investigation was about to pay handsome dividends in that direction. As part of the established enquiry system, reports were required from every constable who had been on duty in Winchester on the fatal night. They yielded little of interest — until PC Michael Pointing returned from weekend leave and was told of the murder. He at once contacted senior detectives with some stunning information.

At about 10.30 pm on the Friday night, he had been stopped on his beat by three young men, one of them a Scot, who enquired whether any pubs were still open. Most pubs in the 1960s closed much earlier than nowadays. PC Pointing said they might try the India Arms and they went on their way.

The constable was still patrolling his beat in the High Street at 1.20 that night when he again saw the Scotsman. This time he was alone. Like a good policeman, PC Pointing approached him and enquired about his movements. MacDonald — for it was he — replied that they had found the India Arms closed but had managed to get into another pub. Where was he going now? He was on his way to Lower

Lower Brook Street in Winchester as it looks today.

Brook Street, he replied — to see a girl he had met in the pub that evening . . .

PC Pointing had blown MacDonald's alibi clear out of the water. The officer's evidence placed the suspect just a couple of hundred yards from the murder scene, at a time when he claimed to have been at his lodgings, within the narrow time frame of Alice Carhart's death, and making his way towards the street where she lived. The investigating officers were jubilant.

More good news came from the fingerprint and forensic experts. Spectrographic comparison between the little key found in MacDonald's room and Mrs Carhart's clock revealed identical striations and wear marks, proving a conclusive link between them. Fingerprint fragments on the Richmond cigarette packet were undoubtedly those of the dead woman, although there were insufficient similarities to satisfy evidential requirements. Best of all, a fingerprint on the door of Mrs Carhart's room had been left there by Willy MacDonald — unquestionably.

At his trial, which lasted four days, MacDonald continued to protest his innocence. Warning the jury that the prosecution case relied solely on 'bits and pieces' of circumstantial evidence, his defence counsel added, 'Very considerable doubt attaches to this case, compelling no doubt superficially, but when probed and scrutinised it is seen to have inconsistencies and weaknesses.'

The jury took an hour and a quarter to reach their verdict. Willy MacDonald was gnawing his lip as they filed back into court. The last words he heard before leaving the dock were those of the judge, Mr Justice Hinchcliffe. 'You have been found guilty by the jury, on evidence which was unmistakable, of the cruel and brutal murder of an old woman. The sentence for non-capital murder is prescribed by law. It is one of life imprisonment.'

CARBON COPY KILLINGS

Detectives and Crown lawyers studied the case papers and agreed that they were dealing with one of the most horrific and unusual murder cases in the Hampshire force's history. No one who had read the witness statements doubted Daniel Rosenthal's guilt. He must have murdered his mother. But did they have sufficient evidence for a conviction? It was a crime he denied and the police had been quite unable to find her body, which was frustrating because the CID always prefer to have a corpse: besides yielding plenty of clues, it is conclusive proof of the victim's death.

There was also the question of his father's disappearance. The evidence that he, too, had been murdered by his son was equally compelling. But Rosenthal wouldn't admit killing his father either, and again the all-important body was missing. So they had two missing persons, two apparent murders, one suspect, no confessions and no bodies.

There was another complication. His American nationality prevented Rosenthal being tried under British law for an alleged murder committed overseas — and father had met his grisly end in France, probably at his Paris flat.

So a bold decision was reached. They would charge Rosenthal with murdering his mother in Hampshire, and help to establish their case by proving that he also murdered his father, in France — the very crime for which the law said he could not be tried. There were other unusual features about Rosenthal's trial. Although the alleged double murderer gave evidence in his own defence, prosecuting counsel chose not to cross-examine him. Not one question. Neither did counsel make his customary closing address to the jury. He let the terrible facts speak for themselves.

Daniel Rosenthal, 27-year-old bachelor and self-styled science student, faced trial in June 1982. He had been arrested the previous September at his two-bedroomed bungalow in Nordik Gardens at Hedge End, to the east of Southampton, where he lived alone. Neighbours in the respectable street, unaware of the horrors yet to be revealed, told one another they weren't surprised the police had taken him, they had always thought he was up to something. Why else were all his curtains kept tightly drawn, day and night? Why did he lead such a reclusive existence, with seemingly not a friend in the world? Their homes were smart; his was neglected, ramshackle and dilapidated. Then there was his weird behaviour — like digging strange holes in the garden with spoons. And what about those rumours of bizarre experiments on chickens? No wonder some people had taken to calling him 'the mad scientist'.

Their flesh would have crept had they seen inside his bungalow. The first police officers to visit, asking questions about his missing mother, were received by a filthy, unkempt and enervated young man. His gloomy home, silent as the grave, was a shambles. An unusual stink pervaded every room. They found chicken feed and chicken wire, with everywhere packets of wire wool, hacksaw blades and a proliferation of rubber gloves. Most chilling, at one end of the darkened lounge stood an eerie false room, a plastic cube about eight feet square, within which Rosenthal reared chickens for dissection and performed macabre experiments with their brains and embryos.

Residents of Nordik Gardens were stunned to hear of the horror uncovered in their street.

In front of this 'laboratory' stood a put-you-up bed where, said Rosenthal, his mother slept during her recent visit. Leah Rosenthal, a wealthy 60-year-old woman, had separated from her husband 11 years previously, although they remained on good terms. He now lived in Paris, she in Israel, whence she travelled to visit a London clinic in late August of 1981.

It was an old friend of the family who had raised the alarm about Leah Rosenthal's disappearance. A multiple sclerosis sufferer, she walked with the aid of crutches, so Dr Fakhir Hussain helped her across London to catch the train from Waterloo to Hampshire, where she was to stay with Danny. Dr Hussain's suspicions were aroused when he telephoned the Hedge End bungalow a few days later to ask why she had not returned to London. 'Mother is not here,' was all Danny Rosenthal would say.

Sufficiently concerned to travel down to Hampshire in person, Dr Hussain had something else to tell the police. Before leaving London, Mrs Rosenthal had telephoned her estranged husband's flat in Paris. His au pair girl, a 21-year-old American named Quibilah Shabazz, took the call. She had some worrying news. She, too, had been to the police. Mr Milton Rosenthal had disappeared for no apparent reason. Miss Shabazz hadn't seen him for nearly two weeks — in fact, not since their son Danny came across to stay with him for a while . . .

Both parents missing and their eccentric son the common link. The two experienced constables who went to Nordik Gardens were deeply suspicious, instinctively discounting Rosenthal's explanation that his mother had left in a taxi after her brief holiday with him. But in the face of his persistent denials it was the brilliant work of Michael Sayce, a senior Home Office forensic scientist, which uncovered the horrifying secrets of that creepy bungalow.

He found minute scraps of human remains in the back bedroom — blood, fatty deposits and fragments of flesh. Furniture in other parts of the house was splashed with blood, as were rubber gloves, skirting boards, walls, a kitchen bucket and bathroom taps. Also in the bathroom, a bed sheet and clothing were heavily bloodstained. Traces on Rosenthal's shoes and trouser bottoms indicated that he had splashed through pools of blood. Most grisly of all, Sayce found an apparently washed hacksaw with a 12-inch blade which under close examination revealed blood, fat and flesh, as if it had sawn through a human body. All these remains came from the same person, said the scientist.

Someone had worked behind those closed curtains, methodically butchering a human being. Where were the pieces now? They were never found. Senior detectives seriously considered whether some of them might have been left in plastic bin-bags for the dustmen. But in the boot of Danny's car there was the macabre evidence of certain maggots which, said experts, could only have got there by feeding on raw flesh. Whose body was it? Discarded among the debris in Rosenthal's metalwork room, police found the sawn-up fragments of a pair of metal crutches — and a tiny label identifying them as his mother's.

Hampshire detectives were by now in touch with their counterparts in Paris, who had drawn a blank in their hunt for the missing father, a 64-year-old retired UNESCO official. But au pair girl Quibilah Shabazz was to reveal something she had previously thought too outlandish to mention — her fears that Daniel Rosenthal had dismembered his father's corpse while she sat barely ten feet away. It happened like this. During Danny's visit to the Paris flat, Miss Shabazz had gone to clean the bathroom. It was locked and Rosenthal told her he was busy in there and should not be disturbed. She decided to do a crossword puzzle in the living room while waiting. For an astonishing two or three hours he kept going backwards and forwards between kitchen and bathroom, occasionally stopping and staring at her. All the time, the bathroom taps were running. 'His father had told me that Daniel had psychological problems,' she said later. 'I thought he was a little weird and doing whatever he wanted in the bathroom, so I left him alone.' Eventually he sent her out for the rest of the day, insisting that he needed privacy.

Next day Milton Rosenthal was nowhere to be found. Danny asked Quibilah for road maps showing the countryside around Paris. And when she did get to clean the bathroom, she found muddy dirt all over the floor, blood-like smears and a plastic bag stuffed with what looked like bloodstained newspapers. It was only grape juice, Rosenthal told her . . .

In a highly unusual concession, the French authorities allowed Hampshire CID officers and British forensic experts to examine the Paris flat. Michael Sayce discovered ample evidence of a most dreadful deed — a carbon copy of the Hedge End horror. Again, a hacksaw was found, bearing tiny particles of human flesh, bone, hair and muscle. There were blood splashes on the floor, walls and ceiling. Part of the floor had been heavily bloodstained, then washed — but blood remained in cracks between the tiles. Blood splashes radiated outwards from the centre of the room. Drag marks in blood led from the living room to the bathroom, whose floor and walls were heavily stained with blood. The whole place had been washed, but blood still marked a sponge and a squeeze mop. Mr Sayce also found fragments of bone.

All these human remains came from the same person. As with the Hedge End butchery, no body parts were found at the scene. Rosenthal still denied killing anybody. He did admit spending those two hours in the Paris bathroom — he said that he had been washing just one pair of underpants and a vest.

As the autumn gave way to winter, and winter to spring, preparations went ahead for Rosenthal's trial on a charge of murdering his mother. A mass of circumstantial evidence was available, including the fact that the bloodstains in Paris and Hedge End matched the groups of Mr and Mrs Rosenthal respectively, but the vexed question remained. Where were their bodies?

Then, in May, just six weeks before the trial began, a French farmer spotted plastic bags and rotting cardboard boxes in his remote field about 100 miles from Paris. He looked inside, and his gruesome discovery resulted in Mr

*Hampshire detectives re-enact their arrest of Rosenthal with an
actor (centre) for a BBC documentary. (Southern Daily Echo)*

Sayce again visiting France, this time to examine parts of
Milton Rosenthal's body. His chest was there but not his
head; sawn off at the base of the neck, it was never found.
In another bag was his pelvis, sawn through from back to
front. Both legs had been sawn off beneath the pelvis. Part
of one leg, sawn off above the foot, was present. So was an
arm, sawn off near the shoulder. Mr Sayce experimented
with the hacksaw found in Paris, concluding that it could
have been used in the dismemberment.

The French field yielded another piece of evidence. One
of the plastic bags came from an English drugstore chain,

Wisebuy. There was a branch in Hedge End, just down the road from Rosenthal's bungalow.

Had this young man really slaughtered both his parents, on quite distinct occasions, before butchering them with such appalling barbarity? Perhaps the answer lay in the strange story he told in the witness box, whispering so softly that he was reminded repeatedly to speak up. A year before the murders he had sent six copies of a long letter to the FBI in America and to New Scotland Yard. It began, 'My parents are dangerous psychotics. They have committed serious crimes against me because they are psychotic.' A later paragraph read, 'I think there is a serious danger that one day [my father] will pay someone to attack me and kill me and make it look like an accident.'

He had lived in absolute terror of his father's hit-men, he told the jury. Now he asked them to believe that it was these villains who for some reason had killed his parents. But might not the jury actually wonder whether his fear had given him the motive for murder? The suggestion, from his own barrister, was rejected by Rosenthal — who had also insisted that his sanity must not be made a trial issue.

He stared at the floor for most of his four-day trial. There was not a flicker of emotion on his face as a unanimous verdict pronounced him guilty of murdering his mother, nor while the judge passed the mandatory life sentence at the conclusion of a thoroughly tragic case.

No one has ever been charged with the murder of Mr Milton Rosenthal.

TWO GRAVE MYSTERIES

There are old people in the village of Herriard who swear the grave has been there for centuries. Why, their grandparents remembered seeing it when they were very small, and they in turn heard the story from their grandparents. It lies alone and originally unmarked in a copse on the edge of Herriard Beeches, not a dozen paces off the Preston Candover road. Whose body rests beneath that simple mound? And whose hands tended it over the years? These were mysteries that excited attention for decades. The woodland grave itself bears no clues. But of one thing folk were sure: the gypsies had something to do with it.

From time to time for as long as anyone could remember, certainly from the early years of the 20th century, passers-by would discover that someone had tidied the grave. Freshly picked wild flowers mysteriously appeared, often in jam jars or milk bottles. Weeds were removed. The undergrowth was cleared back and sometimes a rudimentary cross at the head of the grave would be replaced with another, usually made from twigs of hazel. It only ever happened, said the villagers knowingly, when the gypsies had passed that way — although nobody ever saw them at the grave.

Most people were agreed that a gypsy was buried there. Some said he had been killed in a fight at a farm, others

*The mystery of this lonely woodland grave has finally been solved
— but only in part.*

that he was tried and convicted by a gypsy court for stealing
from one of his own kind, before being hanged in the copse.
Others, though, believed the traveller had committed suicide
after an unfortunate love affair, and they may be nearest the
truth.

Only recently has the mystery been solved, at least in part.
The body, it seems, is that of Jack Haines, a poor itinerant
who for some reason hanged himself in the barn of a nearby
farm, possibly Grange or Merritt's Farm, in about 1860.
Why was he buried in the copse? Still nobody knows.
Perhaps it has something to do with the old custom
forbidding suicides from being laid in consecrated
ground.

As for those mysterious 'gypsy visitors', at least one older resident confessed recently to being among a gang of schoolgirls who secretly cared for the grave during the 1930s and 1940s. Their innocent game took on an added piquancy when the local newspaper carried sober speculation that their wild flowers were actually being placed by gypsies, so they gleefully kept the secret to themselves.

Sometime around 1960 a local couple came across the grave. Initially presuming an animal to be buried there, Mr and Mrs Bill Wyness also began tending the grave and leaving flowers, which surreptitious practice they continued, astonishingly, for more than 30 years. Only when Bill died did his widow reveal their little secret, and only then in order to get help with looking after the grave. Thereafter, until her death in 2000, Peggy Wyness still provided flowers while Herriard Parish Council maintained the now-famous grave, as it does to this day.

So the 'gypsy' myth has been laid to rest. Or has it? Who cared for the Wanderer's Grave before the schoolgirls took over the task in the 1930s? That mystery remains unsolved.

There was never any doubt about who was laid to rest at Southampton's Hollybrook Cemetery on 28 April 1992. Braving hailstones and lashing rain, hundreds of mourners — ordinary members of the public — joined a smattering of showbiz personalities in saying farewell as Benny Hill's coffin was lowered into the grave. At the age of 68, alone in his London flat, the world-famous comedian died of a heart attack. His body was discovered after anxious neighbours who had not seen him for several days persuaded police to break down the door.

Benny was buried in his parents' grave. After the grieving crowds had gone, earth was mounded above the plot, with small flowering plants spelling 'Benny', and so it remained for several months while stonemasons prepared a permanent memorial. But any hopes that he had found his final rest were shattered when an act of pure evil was discovered on 3 October. One of society's most sacred taboos had been broken — the grave had been violated.

The story that first swept through Southampton and beyond was horrifying. Benny Hill's coffin, it was said, had been dug from the ground and smashed open, leaving his shrouded body on the cemetery path. Some versions even said the shroud had been ripped open. Police and cemetery officials moved swiftly to quash these wild rumours. But the truth was bad enough.

Passing the grave at about 8.45 that Saturday morning, a local resident noticed disturbance around the planted mound and on further examination discovered that someone had excavated the grave right down to the coffin. There is some dispute over what else he saw. One usually reliable source claims that the coffin was smashed open and Benny's body, in its burial shroud, could be seen clearly at the bottom of the neatly dug hole. Not so, according to the police. The local superintendent issued a statement: 'An inspection of the scene showed that some persons had dug down to the coffin but that its security had not been breached.' Which, of course, was in itself sufficiently abhorrent to most right-minded people.

After detectives had examined the grave, the lid of the coffin was put back and a concrete slab one foot thick was placed over it to protect against any further depredation. Then the earth was replaced. Finally, a long-term family friend who tended the grave undertook the sad task of restoring the earth mound to its original state, again with 'Benny' spelled out in flowers.

Southampton people were sickened as news of the outrage spread. The *Southern Evening Echo* put three reporters onto the story and ran it over more than two entire pages.

Emotions ran deeper than just natural revulsion at such atrocity. Benny Hill was one of their own. Although their city council had consistently refused to honour him in any way — due, it was often suspected, to socialist doctrinaire disapproval of his style of humour — thousands of Sotonians held Benny in great affection. He himself often expressed pride at his connections with the city of his birth.

Born Alfred Hawthorn Hill in 1924 (he was named after his father, who managed a surgical goods store in Canal Walk), he spent his formative years in Southampton. Right up to the time of his death, despite owning a luxury flat overlooking the Thames in Teddington, London, he often returned to live quietly in his parents' former home, a modest pre-war semi in Westrow Gardens, in the Bannister Park area of Southampton. He promised his mother never to sell the house and he kept his vow.

There was outrage, too, in neighbouring Eastleigh, a town whose civic leaders, unlike their counterparts in the city of his birth, had always been ready to acknowledge its associations with the famous comedian. In the early years of World War II, Eastleigh was where Alfie Hill had some of his first jobs, as a stockroom clerk at Woolworth's and then driving a horse-drawn float as a milk roundsman for a local dairy — the inspiration for his best-selling comic song about Ernie, who 'drove the fastest milk cart in the west'. And it was in and around Eastleigh that the 17-year-old milkman had his first real taste of show business, singing and clowning at functions and clubs with Ivy Lillywhite's little concert party.

Following demobilisation from the Army after the war, Alfie adopted Benny as his stage name, after his hero, the American comedian Jack Benny. His hopes that this would help his career were realised beyond all expectation. Hill's inspired comic routines, for which he personally wrote the songs and scripts, coupled with his astute recognition of the potential of television, made him an international star. At the peak of his fame, a period of many years, he could command his own fee anywhere in the world. In 1990, even after nearly 50 years in show business, Benny Hill's antics could be seen in 97 countries concurrently.

Despite becoming a household name from New Milton to New York by way of Europe, Japan and Australia, the saucy comic genius from Southampton never lost the common touch. Biographers and acquaintances refer repeatedly to his kindness, sincerity, courtesy and lack of pretension. He lived his private life quietly, shunning outrageous publicity stunts. The red-top tabloids struggled to find any dirt to throw at Benny Hill.

Which makes the vile event at Hollybrook Cemetery all the more mysterious. Why should anyone wish to disturb the grave of a man who was held in such affection and whose admirers numbered millions worldwide? What possible motive could there be for such an intrusion on his rest?

In another age, the finger of suspicion would have pointed at the Resurrection Men — the body-snatchers who plundered graves to sell the bodies for dissection by medical students. But this was the late 20th century and such practices were long forgotten. Detectives considered the possibility of a drunken prank, perhaps by students or mindless hooligans. It would not be the first time a famous person's grave had been desecrated as someone's perverted idea of fun.

Other prime candidates for blame might have been ultra-feminists. Benny Hill was never their favourite. Although acknowledged to have been one of the all-time greats of comedy, Hill attracted considerable criticism for his lewd jokes and occasionally smutty routines. He became known

From humble beginnings in Southampton, Benny Hill went on to become an international star.

as King Leer in his own country. In America, despite being enormously popular, they dubbed him the Bawdy Brit. His supporters argue that Hill simply followed a great British tradition of harmless vulgarity, and he himself was always at pains to point out that it was the men, not the women, who were made to look foolish in his sketches. Nevertheless, his constant inclusion of scantily-clad girls, in particular a daring dance group known as Hill's Angels, coupled with saucy comments and innuendo, outraged women's groups and moral crusaders. The advance of political correctness resulted in British television ultimately shunning a comedian whose talent continued to be recognised in many other countries.

But protest during his lifetime had always been passive. There had been none of the militancy displayed towards, for example, the Miss World contest. So the idea of demonstrators waiting more than five months after his death and then resorting to such drastic action seems most unlikely.

A more probable motive surfaced very soon in the investigation. Ever since Hill's funeral a strange rumour had spread around the Southampton area, gaining more credibility with each retelling. Even intelligent people who should have known better were sucked into believing a new urban legend. It had a tenuous basis in fact.

There was no doubt that Benny Hill, a bachelor, had amassed a fortune. Four years before his death a financial magazine said he was worth £10million, on a par with the likes of Sean Connery and Dudley Moore. This revelation — it put Hill among the 200 wealthiest people in Britain — resulted in a page one screamer in *The Sun*, gleefully telling readers that this 'filthy rich' man lived a miser's frugal existence in his 'shabby' Westrow Gardens semi.

Hill was on his own admission a loner. He preferred a

modest lifestyle in which money played little importance. But he was one of the world's most popular entertainers and the cash kept flooding in, from investments and royalties. While he was still warm in his grave, rumour-mongers convinced themselves — and others — that the 'miser' had converted most of his wealth into jewels and precious stones before ordering that they be buried with him in his coffin.

For more than five months the improbable story gained ground. So it was that on a dark October night, callous thieves allowed the lure of easy pickings to overcome any civilised feelings they may have possessed and went digging for a dead man's treasure. The ghouls were within reach of their target when their nerve failed, or perhaps something disturbed their foul purpose, and they slunk off into the night.

Is this the truth behind the mysterious desecration of Benny Hill's grave? If the police had their suspicions, they are not prepared to share them. No one has been prosecuted. Fans from around the world now make their pilgrimage to Hollybrook Cemetery to see where a much-loved but controversial comedian lies buried. And somewhere, probably in Southampton, someone's conscience may yet be troubled by a shameful secret. Perhaps it will haunt them to the grave.

Acknowledgements

It is a pleasure to record my thanks to Botley and Curdridge District Local History Society for allowing me access to their archive material on the history of the Tarbert Fencibles; and to Owen White, who so generously shared the results of his research into the Herriard grave mystery. The valuable assistance given by the *Southern Daily Echo* librarian is also greatly appreciated. Special thanks – as always – to Sandra for her support during this project.